American Sociological Association

Style
GUIDE

Third Edition

Cite as:
American Sociological Association. 2007. *American Sociological Association Style Guide*. 3rd ed. Washington, DC: American Sociological Association.

For information:
American Sociological Association
1430 K Street NW, Suite 600
Washington, DC 20005
(202) 383-9005
E-mail: publications@asanet.org

ISBN 978-0-912764-30-6

Library of Congress Control Number: 2007922267

About the ASA

The American Sociological Association (ASA), founded in 1905, is a nonprofit membership association dedicated to serving sociologists in their work, advancing sociology as a scientific discipline and profession, and promoting the contributions and use of sociology to society. As the national organization for more than 14,000 sociologists, the ASA is well positioned to provide a unique set of benefits to its members and to promote the vitality, viability, and diversity of the discipline. Working at the national and international levels, the Association aims to articulate policy and implement programs likely to have the broadest possible impact for sociology now and in the future.

Publications

ASA publications are key to the Association's commitment to scholarly exchange and wide dissemination of sociological knowledge. ASA publications include 10 journals (described below); substantive, academic, teaching, and career publications; and directories, including the *Directory of Members* and the annual *Guide to Graduate Departments of Sociology*.

The ASA has in place policies and procedures to guide the publications program of the Association. The *Guidelines for the ASA Publications Portfolio*, approved by the ASA Council in 1999, articulates a vision for the publications program and sets forth criteria for the periodic review of ASA journals and the establishment of new journals. A Committee on Publications provides advice and guidance to the ASA Council on the publications program of the Association.

The official journal of the ASA is the *American Sociological Review* (*ASR*), published bimonthly. *ASR* publishes original works of exceptional quality from all areas of sociology. *Contemporary Sociology* (*CS*), also bimonthly, publishes reviews and critical discussions of recent works of sociology and in related disciplines that merit the attention of sociologists.

The Association also publishes six quarterly journals. *Social Psychology Quarterly* (*SPQ*, formerly *Sociometry*) publishes theoretical and empirical papers on the link between the individual and society. The *Journal of Health and Social Behavior* (*JHSB*) publishes sociological analyses of problems of human health and welfare. *Sociology of Education* (*SOE*) is devoted to studies of education as a social institution. *Teaching Sociology* (*TS*) publishes research on the teaching of sociology and presents innovative teaching ideas and strategies. *Sociological Theory* (*ST*) reports on recent developments in all areas of sociological theory. *Contexts*, a journal in magazine format, aims to share sociological research with a broad public.

Sociological Methodology (*SM*), published annually in hardcover format, contains articles of interest to a wide variety of researchers.

Currently, one ASA section (the Community and Urban Sociology Section) also publishes a journal, *City & Community*, which focuses on the sociology of place (especially the metropolis).

The Rose Series in Sociology, published by the Russell Sage Foundation for the ASA, publishes high-visibility, accessible books that integrate ideas and raise controversies across a broad set of sociological fields.

Joining these publications is *Footnotes*, ASA's monthly newsletter, which reports on important issues relating to the discipline, departmental news, activities of the ASA and its Executive Office, and other national and international news relevant to sociology and sociologists.

Table of Contents

3 ASA-Specific Usages and Conventions   37

4 Guidelines for Organizing and Presenting Content   43

5 Guidelines for Using Electronic Resources (E-Resources) 65

6 Preparing and Submitting a Manuscript to an ASA Journal 81

7 Interpreting Copyeditors' Notations   93

8 References and Other Sources   95

Appendix   99

Preface

Over the years, ASA authors and editors have sought consensus on style and format for ASA journals. Editors and managing editors have been concerned that too many authors submitting to ASA journals are uninformed about guidelines for format and style. Authors have been uncertain about what ASA style really is. Is it the same for all ASA journals? Is it the same as *Chicago Manual* style or American Psychological Association style? Does it contain elements of both? Copyeditors have also noted these problems and have added that many authors fail to communicate clearly in their writing.

At the October 1991 meeting of ASA Managing Editors, participants agreed that they should address these problems by providing concrete guidance to authors and editors, specifying the writing style and manuscript organization ASA journals expect. The original draft of this *American Sociological Association Style Guide* was completed in October 1992. It was approved by the ASA Committee on Publications in August 1995 and was first published in 1996. The second edition of the *Style Guide*, published in 1997, incorporated recent style revisions and new information on electronic citations.

This third edition of the *ASA Style Guide* builds on these earlier versions by organizing existing content into a structured system for easier use, expanding guidelines for citing electronic publication sources, and providing examples that illustrate how to apply these guidelines. In keeping with the dramatic changes in publishing over the past decade, a new section has been added on "Guidelines for Using Electronic Resources." In addition, a brief section is now included to cover "ASA-Specific Usages and Conventions," consisting of key rules that have been adopted by the ASA over the years for its internal publications and documents.

Although the *ASA Style Guide* is intended primarily as a reference for authors submitting articles to ASA journals, sociology departments have widely adopted it as a guide for the preparation of theses, dissertations, and other types of research papers. It is also used by professional writers and publishers of scholarly materials on sociological or social science issues more generally. We think that the material in this guide can be applied easily in settings such as these; nevertheless, we have also included a brief section suggesting some basic issues that authors should consider when preparing manuscripts not intended for ASA journals.

In addition, *The Chicago Manual of Style* (2003), on which the *ASA Style Guide* is primarily based, has also grown and changed over the years. This third edition of the *ASA Style Guide* reflects those changes, which are outlined in the section titled "Changes in the *ASA Style Guide* Based on Revisions of *The Chicago Manual of Style*."

Combined with the efforts of the ASA Committee on Publications, the *ASA Style Guide* is based on what editors, managing editors, and copyeditors for ASA journals have observed to be the most common style and format problems in manuscripts accepted for publication. We hope it serves as a useful reference for ASA authors and editors alike.

Sally T. Hillsman
Executive Officer

A Word About the Third Edition of the *ASA Style Guide*

The *ASA Style Guide* highlights and features guidelines for the most common situations encountered by authors and editors in the ASA journal publication process. It is designed to serve as the authoritative reference for writing, submitting, editing, and copyediting manuscripts for ASA journals. In practice, however, the *ASA Style Guide* also serves a wider community of researchers, writers, and publishers who use it to prepare and present scholarly papers in other sociological and social science venues.

The Chicago Manual of Style

Although the *ASA Style Guide* occasionally refers to other style guides and dictionaries, the 15th edition of *The Chicago Manual of Style* (also referred to as *CMOS* in this guide) is the primary reference on which it is based. In addition to the published volume, *The Chicago Manual of Style* offers the following useful resources and tools for writers on its Web site (http://www.chicagomanualofstyle.org/home. html):

- "Chicago-Style Citation Quick Guide" (http://www. chicagomanualofstyle.org/tools_citationguide.html)

- "Electronic Manuscript Preparation Guidelines for Authors" (http://www.press.uchicago.edu/Misc/Chicago/emsguide.html)

- Various other tools (http://www.chicagomanualofstyle. org/tools.html)

Other ASA Resources

In addition to the *Style Guide*, the ASA has other online resources to assist writers. Visit ASA's homepage, http://www.asanet.org, and click on Publications > Journals. On each of the journal homepages, readers will find an Author's Corner with links to helpful writing resources.

New to This Edition

The third edition of the *ASA Style Guide* has been reorganized and expanded to include some key features:

- A numbered system of section heads for easy reference
- A logical arrangement in which guidelines with general application precede specific guidelines for submission of manuscripts to ASA journals
- An enhanced text and an appendix with more examples and illustrations
- Expanded guidelines to bring greater clarity and emphasis to certain issues from previous editions
- A new section on guidelines for preparing manuscripts in general
- A new section on guidelines for electronic sources (including more examples)
- New sections on foreign language and legal usages
- A new section on usages and conventions internal to the ASA (e.g., *Footnotes*, Council, Programs)
- A checklist for submission and transmission of manuscripts to ASA journals

Changes to the *ASA Style Guide* Based on Revisions of *The Chicago Manual of Style*

The ASA reviewed the revisions in *The Chicago Manual of Style*, 15th edition, and has made the following changes to rules in this third edition of the *Style Guide:*

- **Punctuation fonts (Section 2.1):** Preference is now given to setting commas, semicolons, periods, and colons in the font of the preceding text. Question marks and exclamation points are (as before) italic only if they belong to the word they follow. The traditional system is fully acceptable, however (*CMOS* 2003:241–42).

- **Ordinals (Section 2.5):** The forms *2nd* and *3rd* are now generally recommended over *2d* and *3d,* except in legal citation (*CMOS* 2003:381, 665).

- **Capitalizing hyphenated words (Section 2.3):** In titles of works, capitalize only the first element, unless the second element is a proper noun or adjective *(The Dynamic Self-concept: A Social Psychological Perspective;* but *Post-Vietnam War Reconstruction: Challenges for South-East Asia) (CMOS* 2003:368).

- **Plurals of letters (Section 2.1.6):** The plural of single lowercase letters is formed by adding an apostrophe before the *s.* The *s* is roman, even when the letter is italic (e.g., How many *x*'s are there in Exxon?). Capital letters typically do not require an apostrophe in the plural (*CMOS* 2003:295).

- **Ellipsis points (Section 2.1.10):** Although three methods are now offered, the *ASA Style Guide* recommends the "rigorous" method (*CMOS* 2003:458–63).

Other Changes to the *ASA Style Guide*

In addition, the following revisions have been made to style rules in this new edition of the *ASA Style Guide:*

- **Journal issue number (Section 4.3.2):** Previously, the *ASA Style Guide* did not require the journal issue number or month in a reference. The issue number (or month) only needed to be included when necessary to distinguish one issue from another within a volume year (i.e., when each issue in a volume begins with page number 1). In a departure from the second edition, the *ASA Style Guide* now suggests that issue numbers be included as well. If issue numbers are used, they should be used throughout the reference list.

  The form (when used) should be as follows:

  > Kalleberg, Arne L., Barbara F. Reskin, and Ken Hudson. 2000. "Bad Jobs in America: Standard and Nonstandard Employment Relations and Job Quality in the United States." *American Sociological Review* 65(2):256–78.

- **Hyphenations in compound proper nouns denoting ethnicity (Sections 1.2.2; 2.1.3):** *The Chicago Manual of Style* now recommends that no hyphenation be used for these terms (e.g., African American, French Canadian) in either their noun or adjective forms (*CMOS* 2003:304, 325), noting that this issue has been the "subject of considerable controversy, the hyphen being regarded by some as suggestive of bias" (p. 325). Although *CMOS* doubts that the hyphen represents bias, it concludes that the hyphen does not aid in comprehension and can be omitted unless the writer prefers it.

- **Academic degrees (Section 2.8):** Guidelines have been provided regarding acceptable forms of academic degrees.

- **Legal citations and public documents (Section 4.4):**
  A new section has been added with guidelines and examples on how to cite commonly referenced law-related sources and government documents.

- **Ampersands in trademarked titles (Section 4.3.2):**
  Although *The Chicago Manual of Style* suggests that the word *and* be substituted for *&* in titles of works (2003:369, 374) (and ASA journal editors frequently follow this rule), the ASA recommends the use of an ampersand (*&*) if it is part of a trademarked title. Otherwise, editorial discretion is permitted.

- **Volume number in collected works (Section 4.3.2):**
  ASA now recommends a new form that is consistent with citing book volumes generally:

  > Clausen, John A. 1972. "The Life Course of Individuals." Pp. 457–514 in *Aging and Society*. Vol. 3, *A Sociology of Age Stratification*, edited by M. W. Riley, M. Johnson, and A. Foner. New York: Russell Sage.

- **Page numbers in text citations (Section 4.3.1):** The preferred ASA style is *(Kuhn 1970:71)*. Older forms of text citations are not acceptable, for example: *(Kuhn 1970, p. 71)*.

- **Guidelines for the preparation of manuscripts in general (Section 4.9):** Because the *ASA Style Guide* has been adopted as a standard for preparation of other types of manuscripts (e.g., sociological dissertations and theses), information is provided on some key elements of preparing manuscripts in general.

1 ASA Editorial Style

The *ASA Style Guide* aims to achieve several goals:

- To establish uniformity and consistency in style among ASA publications with respect to elements such as formats for text citations, references, and other structural features. The guidelines established here assist editors and copyeditors to implement uniform standards across all ASA journals in their final published forms.

- To provide an authoritative reference source on style issues for authors who are writing manuscripts for ASA journals. This *ASA Style Guide* is primarily based on *The Chicago Manual of Style* (*CMOS*) but departs from the *CMOS* on certain points. The guidelines presented here provide acceptable stylistic forms (e.g., how to cite chapters in books in a reference list) for ASA journals.

- To summarize basic issues on effective writing for authors in general. Elements of effective, polished writing (e.g., rules of good syntax and grammar, conventionally accepted usages and spellings of words, correct use of punctuation) are summarized in a portable format for use by writers in a wide variety of settings. The *ASA Style Guide* is structured so it can be easily adapted for other purposes (e.g., as a teaching tool or for ASA Web site development).

1.1 Style Matters

The *Merriam-Webster's Collegiate Dictionary* defines *style* as "a distinctive manner of expression . . . a particular manner or technique by which something is done, created, or performed" (2003). Style thus encompasses organizational constraints, professional requirements, and writers' inclinations and preferences.

1.2 ASA Style

1.2.1 Some Basics

In addition to guidelines for presentation formats (e.g., headings, tables, figures, citations, and references), the *ASA Style Guide* provides some basic information on the mechanics of writing (e.g., correct syntax, grammar, punctuation, spelling, word usage). Attention to these issues will certainly enhance writing style, but it is important to note that communicating effectively in writing depends on the more fundamental thinking-and-planning stage, which involves conceptualizing ideas; conducting solid, objective, accurate analysis; developing a strong thesis or point of view; organizing materials and citing them in a systematic way; "mapping" the ideas in a logical and coherent manner; and developing a design or outline for presentation in the manuscript.

Guidelines for reporting on empirical social science, such as the "Standards for Reporting on Empirical Social Science Research in AERA Publications," recently published in *Educational Researcher,* highlight some basic issues pertaining to the design and analyses phases of a writing effort (AERA 2007). A volume by Day and Gastel, titled *How to Write and Publish a Scientific Paper* (2006), also provides valuable insights and guidance on the basic elements of organizing, writing, and publishing scientific papers.

The *ASA Style Guide* emphasizes formal, objective, orderly, and grammatically sound expression. For example, writers should generally avoid writing in the first person, injecting opinion, overstating claims, and overwriting. They should use the active voice, maintain consistency in grammatical constructions, be concrete and specific, aim for creative but smooth composition, and follow standard usages and conventions. Scholarly writing should reflect both intellectual and stylistic rigor.

1.2.2 Plagiarism

The ASA has a firm commitment to full and proper attribution and authorship credit, as set forth in the *ASA Code of Ethics*, in Section 14 on plagiarism:

> (a) In publications, presentations, teaching, practice, and service, sociologists explicitly identify, credit, and reference the author when they take data or material verbatim from another person's written work, whether it is published, unpublished, or electronically available.
>
> (b) In their publications, presentations, teaching, practice, and service, sociologists provide acknowledgment of and reference to the use of others' work, even if the work is not quoted verbatim or paraphrased, and they do not present others' work as their own whether it is published, unpublished, or electronically available.

Other sections of the *ASA Code of Ethics* define ethical responsibilities of authors in other areas, such as authorship credit, the publication process, and responsibilities of reviewers. (See the *ASA Code of Ethics*, available at http://www.asanet.org.)

1.2.3 Clarity

The essential element of good style and effective writing is clarity of expression, both with respect to ideas and structure. Several volumes by Williams, including the recently published *Style: Lessons in Clarity and Grace* (2007), emphasize the importance of clarity, coherence, and concision in effective prose and elegant, polished writing. Clarity in writing means using direct and straightforward language; expressing ideas accurately in jargon-free, uncluttered phrases; and adhering to a well-designed outline. Writing clearly also involves a focus on "nuts-and-bolts" issues (such as consistency of verb tenses, accuracy in spelling, correct word usages, and correct punctuation) that are key to effective presentation. Authors are encouraged to think of themselves as both authors and editors (Becker 1986) and should submit manuscripts for publication only after multiple careful readings and revisions.

1.2.4 Bias

In keeping with ASA's firm commitment to promoting inclusivity and diversity in all areas, the *ASA Style Guide* strongly urges the avoidance of language reflecting bias or stereotyping on the basis of gender, race, ethnicity, disabilities, sexual orientation, family status, religion, or other personal characteristics. For more ideas on how to approach gender-neutral and bias-free expression, refer to *The Chicago Manual of Style* (2003:157, 233), the fifth edition of the *Publication Manual of the American Psychological Association* (2001:66–76), and that association's Web sites: http://www.apastyle.org/disabilities.html, http://www.apastyle.org/sexuality.html, and http://www.apastyle.org/race.html.

Gender

Unless gendered terms are specific to analysis of data or demographics, use nongendered terms such as *person, people, individual,* or *humankind* rather than *man, men,* or *mankind.* There are a number of common techniques for maintaining a gender-neutral approach:

- Rephrase the sentence (change *a boy or girl lives in that house* to *a child lives in that house*).

- Use a plural noun or pronoun (*people, they*).

- Replace the gendered pronoun with an article (change *his* to *the*).

- Delete the pronoun (change *avoid his bias* to *avoid bias*).

In general, avoid slashed gendered terms (*he/she*, *him/her*, *his/hers*), repetition of the conjunction *or* (*he or she*, *her or him*, *his or hers*), and switching gender order (using *he* or *she* and then using *she* or *he*).

Some writers may wish to distinguish the use of terms relating to gender and sexuality (*woman, female, gender*) for accuracy and precision. The author should note such preferences when submitting a manuscript for publication.

The American Heritage Dictionary of the English Language (2000) also provides suggestions for gender-neutral language in a usage note that follows the entry for *he*.

Race and Ethnicity

The classification and terminology of race and ethnicity are complex and have changed over time. Avoid racial and ethnic stereotyping of groups. Authors using racial and ethnic terms should aim to be as specific and precise as possible when identifying a person's origin or group. For example, *Cuban* is more specific than *Hispanic*; *Japanese* is more specific than *Asian*.

Use the following:

- African American (no hyphen) (*CMOS* 2003:304, 325)
- black (not capitalized)
- white (not capitalized)
- Hispanic, Chicano, Latino, Latina (use *Latino* or *Latina* if gender is known; use *Latino* if gender is unknown or known to be male)
- American Indian, Native American (no hyphen)
- Asian or Asian American (no hyphen)

Avoid the following:

- Afro-American
- Negro
- Oriental

For further explanation, refer to *The Chicago Manual of Style* (2003:233, 325) and to the *Publication Manual of the American Psychological Association* (2001:67–69, 74–75).

1.2.5 Verbs

The *ASA Style Guide* focuses on some basic rules of grammar relating to verbs. Information about rules governing other parts of speech (nouns, pronouns, adjectives, adverbs, prepositions, and interjections) is covered in Chapter 5 of *The Chicago Manual of Style* (2003:147–95).

Active Voice

Because the active voice is more precise and less wordy, use it whenever possible. The subject of an active sentence tells the reader who did something, and the active verb says what happened. A passive sentence tells the reader what happened but attributes the action to no one. For example:

> *Passive voice:* Three hundred fifty college graduates between the ages of 25 and 35 were queried.

> *Active voice:* A team of 14 trained interviewers queried 350 college graduates between the ages of 25 and 35.

Avoid the passive voice by saying *The authors found . . .* rather than *It was found . . .*, or by using the first person (*I* or *we*) in text. ASA style discourages the use of the personal pronoun in formal writing.

> *Passive voice:* All 350 interview transcripts were analyzed.

> *Active voice:* The analysis included all 350 interview transcripts.

Tense—Past or Present?

Most problems with verb tense result from inconsistency. Different sections of a paper can use different verb tenses, but within each section, the tense should be the same.

For literature reviews: In general, use the past tense. In discussing past research, use the tense that communicates that the research has been completed:

> In their study on education and income, Smith and Jones (1994) found that the college graduates in their sample earned more over the life course than did high school graduates.

However, mixing past and present tense within a sentence sometimes better communicates a finding from past research:

> Jones (1969) concluded that students are more likely to cohabit than they are to marry.

In this case, Jones's conclusion is understood to be timeless—as correct today as it was when she completed her study.

In the methods section: Use the past tense to describe the methods used to conduct a study:

> We completed our interviews in the spring of 1992.

In the results section: Use either past or present tense:

> The results support our hypothesis.

> The results supported our hypothesis.

See Day and Gastel (2006:191–93) for use of tense in scientific writing.

Subject–Verb Agreement

The subject of a sentence must agree in number with the predicate verb, regardless of the words or phrases that come between them. Certain subject–verb constructions, however, often present problems:

- The word *data* is plural and takes a plural verb:

    The data, as reported in the appendix, are correct.

- Collective nouns (*committee, faculty*) may take either a plural (if referring to individuals) or a singular (if referring to a group) verb. Context determines the appropriate use:

    The faculty is meeting this afternoon.

    The faculty are voting on the issue later today.

- Words such as *none, some, any, most, part,* and *number* take either a plural or singular verb, depending on the context. A suggestion by *The Chicago Manual of Style* may be a useful guide: If the word is followed by a singular noun, treat it as a singular; if by a plural noun, treat it as a plural (2003:222):

    None of the report was printed.

    None of the students were in attendance.

1.2.6 Wordy Phrases

Some commonly used words and expressions can weigh down writing. Simplify and enhance writing by using "plain" language. The following list, adapted from Appendix 2 of Day and Gastel (2006:265–72), presents common wordy phrases and suggests alternative expressions. Reading this list should increase sensitivity to unnecessary words typically used in writing.

Wordy	*Better*
a considerable amount of	much
a considerable number of	many
a great deal of	much
a majority of	most
a number of	a few, several, many, some
absolutely essential	essential
accounted for by	because, due to, caused by
add the point that	add that
adjacent to	near
along the lines of	like
an example of this is the fact that	for example
an order of magnitude faster	10 times faster
analyzation	analysis
another aspect of the situation	as for
are of the opinion that	think that, believe
are of the same opinion	agree
as a matter of fact	in fact [or omit]
as in the case	as happens
as of this date	today
as per	[omit]
as regards	about
as related to	for, about
as to	about [or omit]
at a rapid rate	rapidly
at an earlier date	previously
at some future time	later
at the conclusion of	after
at the present writing [or time]	now
at this point in time	now
based on the fact that	because
by means of	by, with
causal factor	cause
collect together	collect
completely full	full
concerning, concerning the nature of	about
consensus of opinion	consensus
considerable amount of	much
definitely proved	proved

Wordy	*Better*
demonstrate	show, prove
despite the fact that	although
due to the fact that	because, since
during the course of	during, while
during the time that	while
enclosed herewith	enclosed
end result	result
endeavor	try
entirely eliminate	eliminate
eventuate	happen
except in a small number of cases	usually
exhibit a tendency to	tend to
fatal outcome	death
few [many] in number	few [many]
fewer in number	fewer
finalize	end
first of all	first
firstly [secondly, etc.]	first [second, etc.]
for the purpose of	for, to
for the reasons that	because, since
from the point of view of	for
future plans	plans
give an account of	describe
give rise to	cause
has been engaged in a study of	has studied
has the capability of	can
have an input into	contribute to
have in regard to	about
have the appearance of	look like
if at all possible	if possible
impact [verb]	affect
important essentials	essentials
in a number of cases	some
in a position to	can, may
in a satisfactory manner	satisfactorily
in a very real sense	in a sense [or omit]
in almost all instances	nearly always
in case, in case of	if

Wordy	*Better*
in close proximity	close, near
in connection with	about, concerning
in favor of	for, to
in light of the fact that	because
in many cases	often
in my opinion it is not an unjustifiable assumption that	I think
in reference [with reference to, in regard to]	about
in order to	to
in rare cases	rarely
in relation to	toward, to
in relation with	with
in respect to	about
in some cases	sometimes
in terms of	about, in, for [or omit]
in the absence of	without
in the case of	[can usually omit]
in the case that	if, when
in the course of	during
in the event that	if
in the first place	first
in the majority of instances	usually
in the matter of	about
in the nature of	like
in the neighborhood of	about
in the normal course of our procedure	normally
in the not-too-distant future	soon
in the opinion of this writer	in my opinion, I believe
in the possession of	has, have, owned by
in the vicinity of	near
in view of the above, in view of the foregoing circumstances, in view of the fact that	therefore, because
inasmuch as	as, because
incline to the view	think
involve the necessity of	require
is defined as	is [will frequently suffice]

Wordy	*Better*
it has been reported by Smith	Smith reported
it is apparent that	apparently
it is believed that	I believe
it is clear [obvious] that	therefore, clearly [obviously]
it is observed that	[omit]
it is often the case that	often
it is our conclusion in the light of the investigation that	we conclude that, our findings indicate that
it should be noted that X	X
it stands to reason	[omit]
it was noted that if	if
it would not be unreasonable to assume	I [we] assume
leaving out of consideration	disregarding
make an examination of	examine
not of a high order of accuracy	inaccurate
not withstanding the fact	although
of considerable magnitude	big, large, great
of very minor importance [import]	unimportant
on a few occasions	occasionally
on account of the conditions described	because of the conditions
on account of the fact that	because
on the ground that	because
perform an analysis of	analyze
presently	now
prior to, in advance of	before
proceed to investigate [study, analyze]	investigate [omit proceed to]
relative to this	about this
resultant effect	effect
subsequent to	after
taking this factor into consideration, it is apparent that	therefore, therefore it seems
that is, i.e.	[usually can be omitted if phrase or clause to which it refers has been written clearly]
the data show that X	X

Wordy	Better
the existence of	[usually can be omitted]
the foregoing	the, this, that, these, those
the fullest possible extent	[omit, or use most, completely, or fully]
the only difference being	except
the question as to whether or not	whether
there are not very many to be considered	few
to be sure	of course
to summarize the above	in sum, in summary
under way	begun, started
with reference [regard, respect] to	[omit, or use about]
with the exception of	except
with the result that	so that
with this in mind, with this in mind it is clear that	therefore

1.2.7 Common Misusages

Under a section titled "Glossary of Troublesome Expressions," *The Chicago Manual of Style* lists dozens of words that are commonly misused (2003:196–233). The following list includes a few of these:

Affect; effect
Affect in the verb form means to influence; *effect* is used as a noun to mean result. *Effect* can also be used as a verb meaning to bring about or to make happen.

Altogether; all together
Altogether means wholly or completely; *all together* refers to the same time or place.

Assure; ensure; insure
To *assure* is to state confidently; to *ensure* is to make sure or certain; to *insure* is to protect against financial loss.

Between; among
As a general guideline, *between* indicates a one-on-one relationship (*between you and me*), while *among* indicates collective or

undefined relationships (*honor among thieves*). *Between* can also be used with groups of three or more if the statement refers to multiple one-on-one relationships (*trade between the United States, Mexico, and Canada*).

Biannual; semiannual; biennial
Biannual and *semiannual* both mean occurring twice a year; *biennial* means taking place once in two years.

Can; may
Can refers to physical or mental ability; *may* indicates possibility or permission.

Compliment; complement
A *compliment* is a flattering remark; a *complement* is something that is required to supply a deficiency.

Due to; because of
Due to is interchangeable with *attributable to*; *because of* means for the reason that.

Elicit; illicit
Elicit (verb) means to draw out (an answer); *illicit* (adjective) means improper or unlawful.

Emigrate; immigrate
To *emigrate* is to leave one's country to settle in another one; to *immigrate* is to come into a country of which one is not a native.

Its; it's
Its is the possessive form of *it* (belonging to it); *it's* is the contraction for *it is*.

Lay; lie
Lay means to set down (it is a transitive verb requiring a direct object): *Lay the clothes on the bed*. *Lie* means to assume a position of rest: *Lie down for a nap*.

Less; fewer
Less refers to degree, value, or amount; *fewer* is used to compare numbers or countable things.

That; which

Use *that* in restrictive (defining) clauses—clauses that define or restrict the meaning of the subject or the main clause (*The data that came from the university were crucial to our study*). Restrictive clauses are not set off by commas. In general, if either *that* or *which* can be used, *that* is preferable.

Use *which* for nonrestrictive (nondefining) clauses—clauses that do not change the meaning of the subject or main clause but simply add information about something already identified. Nonrestrictive clauses always use *which* and must be set off by commas or parentheses because such clauses are indeed parenthetical (*The data, which came from several different sources, are available on request from the authors*).

Who; whom

Who is used as a subject of the verb or a predicate nominative (*Fido, who barks constantly, annoys the neighbors*); *whom* is used as the object of a verb or a preposition (*To whom should these papers be sent?*).

2 Some Mechanics of Style

Effective writing requires attention to conventions and rules for punctuation, spelling, syntax, and grammar. Summaries of basic issues are included in grammar and style guides, including in Day and Gastel (2006:188), Strunk and White (2000), and Williams (2007). Writers should:

- Check that pronouns agree with antecedents.
- Pay attention to case (*between you and me* is correct).
- Avoid ending sentences with prepositions.
- Check that verbs agree with subjects (*The data are included in the report*).
- Use consistent verb tenses.
- Avoid:
    - Double negatives
    - Split infinitives
    - Sentence fragments
    - Dangling phrases or misplaced modifiers
- Check for consistency in sentence structure.

2.1 Punctuation

Punctuation is used to clarify expression in writing and to make reading easier. Follow these general punctuation guidelines:

- Use only one space after all punctuation (including between sentences). Periods and colons should not be followed by two spaces.
- All punctuation marks should be in the same font (roman or italic) as the preceding text (*CMOS* 2003:241) (e.g., The man in the restaurant shouted,

"*Fire!*"). (*Note:* This is a departure from previous usage in *The Chicago Manual of Style*.)

2.1.1 Commas

Commas indicate a slight pause in a sentence. Use commas:

- **To separate items in a series.** When listing three or more words, phrases, or clauses in a series, use a comma before the conjunction joining the last two:

    He gathered data on their cultural, educational, and socioeconomic backgrounds.

- **After an adverbial or participial phrase at the beginning of a sentence:**

    Importantly, low-income women benefited from the program.

    According to several studies, the employment rate grew modestly in the last quarter.

    Grabbing a book off the shelf, she slipped out the door.

- **After introductory phrases when needed for clarity:** Both of the following examples are understandable and correct:

    In 1991, the GNP dropped once again.

    In 1991 the GNP dropped once again.

- **Before a conjunction that joins two independent clauses:**

    The interviewers introduced themselves, and then they answered the subjects' questions.

    Note: Do not use a comma before a conjunction joining two parts of a complex predicate:

    The interviewers introduced themselves and answered the subjects' questions.

- **After certain abbreviations (i.e., e.g.,):**

  She attended a number of Africa-themed sessions (i.e., those highlighting the work of sociologists working on issues related to Africa).

  The presentation explored the range of women's work in different areas (e.g., science, technology, service work).

- **To set off elements in dates:**

  January 19, 1968

  January 19, 1968, was the correct date.

  But:

  We collected data during January 1968.

2.1.2 Semicolons and Colons

Semicolons are used to separate major coordinating elements of a sentence, such as independent clauses in a compound sentence. A colon marks a major division in a sentence or is used to indicate an elaboration of what precedes it.

Use a semicolon to:

- **Separate two independent clauses not joined by a conjunction.** Semicolons connect two related clauses more powerfully than do conjunctions:

  The results are unequivocal; the contemporary attitude toward the future is pessimistic.

- **Separate elements in a sentence already separated by commas:**

  Of these, 80 percent were employed in institutions of higher education; 14 percent worked in federal, state, or local governments; and 3 percent owned businesses that employed others.

Use a colon to indicate that what follows is an amplification of what precedes it:

- **Separate elements or elements in a series amplifying what preceded the colon:**

    The soldier was faced with the following problems: how to get rid of his parachute and how to contact an ally.

- **Begin the sentence after the colon with a capital letter when the colon follows a complete clause and introduces a complete sentence:**

    The results were as follows: The men interrupted the women in 25 percent of the professional exchanges, but the women seldom interrupted the men.

    But:

    The codebook included four key variables: race/ethnicity, gender, age, and education.

- **Lists of important points are often numbered in the text.** Such lists typically are introduced by an independent clause followed by a colon and then by a series of numbered statements. Use commas to separate numbered lists consisting of simple phrases; use semicolons to separate numbered lists of complex phrases or clauses:

    Three firm-level attributes distinguish one firm from another: (1) the size of the firm, (2) the age of the firm, and (3) whether the firm is connected to the financial or industrial sector.

    Three firm-level attributes distinguish one firm from another: (1) the size of the firm, measured by number of employees in 1992; (2) the age of the firm, measured in 1992 by the number of years since incorporation; and (3) whether the firm is connected to the financial, industrial, or service sector.

- **Use a colon to separate year and page information or volume (and issue) and page numbers in text citations and references:**

    Text: (Duster 2006:1–5)

    Reference:
    Duster, Troy. 2006. "Comparative Perspectives and Competing Explanations: Taking on the Newly Configured Reductionist Challenge to Sociology." *American Sociological Review* 71(1):1–15.

2.1.3 Hyphens and Dashes

A hyphen is indicated by a -, without spaces before or after, as in *cross-national*. A dash is indicated by two hyphens (--) or an em dash (—) without spaces before, after, or in-between, as in *He belonged to many organizations—ASA and APA among them.*

Use hyphens in:

- **Compound adjectives** (*never-married men, family-based finances, middle-class families*).

- **Compound nouns and numbers** (*great-granddaughter, thirty-eight*), unless they otherwise are more readable and understandable as a single word (*policymaker*).

- **Electronic resources following the abbreviation** *e* for *electronic* (*e-mail, e-commerce, e-journal*). (See Section 5.1 for additional guidelines and examples of hyphenation for electronic materials.)

- **To separate a campus name from an institution:**

    University of Wisconsin-Madison

    University of Illinois-Chicago

    But: When the campus location is hyphenated, use the following form:

    University of Illinois at Urbana-Champaign

Do not hyphenate:

- Words beginning with *non, pre,* and other such prefixes (*nonfarm, precontrol*) unless the prefix precedes a proper noun (*non-Hispanic*).

- Compound proper names designating ethnicity: *African American, French Canadians* (*CMOS* 2003:304, 325).

See *The Chicago Manual of Style* (2003:299–308) for additional examples and more information on using hyphens in compound words and with prefixes.

See Section 2.3 on how to capitalize hyphenated words in a title.

2.1.4 Em Dashes

An em dash is equal to the width of a capital *M*. Indicate an em dash by typing two consecutive hyphens or by entering the symbol from the character set in word processing software. Use an em dash to signify a break in thought that causes an abrupt change in a sentence, to add an explanatory clause or phrase, or to set off parenthetical elements. (See *CMOS* 2003:260–65.)

> Each of the three variables—education, income, and family size—is considered separately.

Three em dashes followed by a period (———.) in a reference list or bibliography means the publication has the same author or editor as the preceding entry.

2.1.5 En Dashes

An en dash is equal to the width of a capital *N* (and is half the width of an em dash). (Check the word processing software documentation for instructions on how to key the en dash.)

Use en dashes in:

- **Citations and references to indicate ranges of pages in a book or journal:**

    See Johnson (1994:122–35) for additional information.

- **Text or tables as a minus or negative sign:**

    During the last two years, we have experienced an average annual temperature change of –2 degrees.

- **Tables, to indicate ranges of dates or variables:**

    Income 1952–1960

    In text, however, use *to* or *through* to express ranges of years, values for variables, and so on:

    We used the income data from 1952 to [or through] 1960.

2.1.6 Apostrophes

- Form the **possessive** for proper names and singular nouns by adding an apostrophe and *s,* as in *student's, Congress's, Cox's,* and *Parsons's* (exceptions include *Jesus'* and *Moses'*). See *The Chicago Manual of Style* (2003:281–86) for additional examples.

- Form the **possessive of a plural noun** that ends in *s* by adding an apostrophe only, as in *witches' recipes* and *students' transcripts.*

- Use apostrophes to form **contractions**—*can't, isn't,* and so on. Do not use contractions in formal writing unless they are part of quotations.

- Form the **plural of single lowercase letters by adding an apostrophe before the *s.*** The *s* is roman, even when the letter being pluralized is italic. Capital letters normally do not require an apostrophe in the plural

(*CMOS* 2003:295). (*Note:* This is new in the 15th edition of *CMOS*.)

How many *x*'s are there in Exxon?

2.1.7 Quotation Marks

Use quotation marks to:

- **Reproduce direct, verbatim text or other quoted material:**

    "There are lots of challenges," Major Murray said.

    The president indicated that "the economy has improved in the last quarter."

    Note: No comma is needed after *that, whether*, or similar conjunctions.

- **Set off the title of an article or chapter in a book in a reference list:**

    Martinez, Ramiro F., Jr. 1996. "Latinos and Lethal Violence: The Impact of Poverty and Inequality." *Social Problems* 43(2):131–46.

- **Emphasize sarcasm, irony, or humor:**

    The "furnished apartment" was one room with a bare light bulb over a mattress on the floor.

    Note: Avoid overuse of this technique; if the irony or humor is obvious, there is usually no need to highlight it with quotation marks.

- **Denote invented terminology:**

    The company restricted certain employees from "IMing" customers or suppliers.

See also Chapter 11 of *The Chicago Manual of Style* (2003:270, 444–71) for other aspects of use of quotation marks and how to cite quoted material.

Note: Generally, punctuation appears inside quotation marks, such as *"this,"* and *"that."* Quotation marks appear before a semicolon (e.g., *". . .this";*).

2.1.8 Quoted Material

- **Quotations in text** begin and end with quotation marks; the author, date, and/or page numbers follow the end-quote and precede the period:

   Wright and Jacobs (1994) found that "the variation in men's earnings relative to their peers in the labor force was not a reliable predictor of men's . . . flight from feminizing occupations" (p. 531).

   or

   One study found that "the variation in men's earnings relative to their peers in the labor force was not a reliable predictor of men's . . . flight from feminizing occupations" (Wright and Jacobs 1994:531).

- **Block quotations** are set off in a separate, indented paragraph and should be used for longer quotations (generally, 50 words or more). Block quotations should not be enclosed in quotation marks.

   As stated by Wright and Jacobs (1994):

   The variation in men's earnings relative to their peers in the labor force was not a reliable predictor of men's attrition. This finding is inconsistent with the prediction that declines in earnings are responsible for male flight from feminizing occupations. (P. 531)

   Note: The author, date, and/or page number follows the period in a block quotation and the *"P"* for *"page"* is capitalized when the page number is cited alone without author and date information, as in the above example.

2.1.9 Parentheses and Brackets

Parentheses set off information that is interjected or less closely related to the rest of the sentence, while brackets enclose words added by a writer to distinguish those from the original author being quoted.

Use parentheses to:

- **Set off less important information:**

  The proportion of children living in one-parent (mother-only) families increased.

- **Enclose acronyms or citations in text:**

  The Panel Study of Income Dynamics (PSID)

  (Bursik and Grasmick 1993)

Use brackets to:

- **Enclose material included within parentheses:**

  (See also the discussion in Bowers [1985] and Bureau of Justice Statistics data [1999].)

- **Enclose material inserted by someone other than the original author:**

  "Higher rates of MS [multiple sclerosis] were found in cold climates."

  "[N]ationally representative social surveys . . . indicate that institutionalization is common."

- **Enclose an earlier published source:**

  Veblen ([1899] 1979) stated that . . .

2.1.10 Ellipses

The Chicago Manual of Style (2003:458–63) specifies several methods for placing ellipses. ASA style uses the **"rigorous" method,** in which one period signifies a true period, and any change to the original quote is indicated in brackets (see also preceding Section 2.1.9). Observe the following conventions in placing ellipses:

- Insert a space after every period. (Do not use the ellipses character automatically set by word processing software.)

- Locate all periods on the same line if ellipses fall at the end of a line.

- Place brackets around any change in punctuation.

- Denote missing information with a space followed by a period. Therefore, in the example on the following page, the fourth period before the text beginning "Here I have lived a quarter of a century" is the true period. Also, the sentence following the first set of ellipses begins with a capital letter, indicating the beginning of a new sentence.

Use ellipses to:

- **Represent missing information, including whole sentences.**

  The text of the "Farewell Address" by Abraham Lincoln to his friends and neighbors in Springfield, Illinois, on February 11, 1861, is as follows:

  > My friends, no one, not in my situation, can appreciate my feeling of sadness at this parting. To this place, and the kindness of these people, I owe everything. Here I have lived a quarter of a century, and have passed from a young to an old man. Here my children have been born, and one is buried. I now leave, not knowing when, or whether ever, I may return, with a task before me greater than that which rested upon Washington. Without the assistance of the Divine Being who ever attended him, I cannot succeed. With that assistance I cannot fail. Trusting in Him who can go with me, and remain with you, and be everywhere for good, let

us confidently hope that all will yet be well. To His care commending you, as I hope in your prayers you will commend me, I bid you an affectionate farewell.

The following sentences are shortened from the preceding text as follows:

My friends, no one, not in my situation, can appreciate my feeling of sadness at this parting. . . . Here I have lived a quarter of a century . . . [and] [h]ere my children have been born, and one is buried. . . .

- **Represent missing information at the beginning or end of quotations** (*CMOS* 2003:463). Use three ellipsis points for a quote that begins with a capitalized word (such as a proper name) that was not at the beginning of a sentence in the original:

    . . . President Carter announced to his cabinet that he would find out what went wrong; in the meantime, the Commission continued its investigation.

If the final words of the quoted sentence are omitted, place 4 periods (all spaced, including the first) after the quoted material:

    These findings are part of a larger mosaic of knowledge about the impact of immigration on children . . . .

2.2 Spelling

ASA uses the 11th edition of *Merriam-Webster's Collegiate Dictionary* (2005) to determine correct spelling and usage. In general, writers are encouraged to use a standard dictionary when writing or preparing papers or presentations. (ASA editors may inquire about which dictionary an author used in preparation of a manuscript submitted to them.)

If the dictionary lists two or more spellings for a word, use the first spelling (*benefited* rather than *benefitted*, *focused* rather than *focussed*, *toward* rather than *towards*).

Spell out words such as *percent*, *versus*, and *chi-square* in running text.

See Section 2.9 for foreign word usages.

See Section 5.1 for preferred spelling for electronic resources.

2.3 Capitalization

Use the following guidelines for capitalization:

- In the **titles of books and articles,** capitalize the first word in the title or subtitle and all words except prepositions (*of, onto, between, through*), articles (*a, an, the*), and coordinating conjunctions (*and, but, or*).

  "Provisional Distribution of the Population of the United States into Psychological Classes"

  "Provisional Distribution of the Population of the United States: Psychological Classifications"

- Capitalize the **names of racial and ethnic groups** that represent geographical locations or linguistic populations (*Hispanic, Asian, African American, Appalachian*). (See *CMOS* 2003:325–26 for additional examples.)

- Do not capitalize **black** and **white** when designating racial groups.

- Capitalize references to **regions of the United States,** such as the *South*, the *North*, the *Midwest*, when referring to places. Capitalize *Southerners* and *Northerners* only when referring to the Civil War; lowercase groups such as *northerners, southerners,* and *midwesterners*. Do not capitalize *north, south, east,* and *west* when referring to directions. The adjectival forms of words (*midwestern states, southern industry*) are not capitalized.

- In titles of works, **capitalize only the first element of a hyphenated word, unless the second element is a proper noun or adjective** (*The Dynamic Self-concept: A Social Psychological Perspective* but *Post-Vietnam War Reconstruction: Challenges for South-East Asia*). (*Note:* This is a new rule in the 15th edition of the *CMOS* 2003:358.)

- **Capitalize words associated with proper nouns:**

  > Council also appointed a Subcommittee on ASA Policymaking and Resolutions, chaired by Patricia Roos. . . . In January 2000, Council asked the Subcommittee to continue its work for another year.

- Do not capitalize the word *the* in running text for **institutional titles** such as *the University of Chicago, the University of Texas System, the University of Wisconsin-Madison* (*CMOS* 2003:338). When the campus location is hyphenated, use the following form: University of Illinois at Urbana-Champaign.

  Note: Institutional names are spelled out in full.

2.4 Italics

Use italics for emphasis (but be careful to use them sparingly) and to highlight terms in specific contexts, to identify certain foreign words, and for titles of books, periodicals, movies, radio and TV show names, and other formally published material.

2.5 Numbers

Questions frequently arise regarding conventions for spelling out numbers versus using numerals. Following are the general rules for use of numbers in text:

- Spell out numbers one through nine.

- Use numerals for numbers 10 or greater.

- Follow the same pattern for ordinal numbers. (Spell out numbers less than 10: *first, second, ninth*; but *10th, 44th.*)

- Always spell out numbers at the beginning of a sentence. (If possible, however, do not begin a sentence with a number.)

- Use numerals for references to tables, figures, hypotheses, and so on (*Figure 1, Table 3*).

- Spell out centuries: *nineteenth century, twenty-first century.*

- Spell out common fractions (*two-thirds majority; reduced by one half*).

Note: The forms *2nd* and *3rd* are now generally recommended over *2d* and *3d* except in legal citation (*CMOS* 2003:381, 665).

Examples:

> One hundred twenty-four suspects avoided capture by the 14 officers.
>
> They completed nine interviews during the first morning.
>
> Table 3 presents a summary of results.
>
> the 95th percentile

In text citations and reference lists, indicate inclusive page numbers with an en dash (see 2.1.5). Most page references (except for *pp. 102–106, pp. 1101–1108*, and the like) should be elided (*pp. 132–48, pp. 1002–11, pp. 1054–82*). (See *CMOS* 2003:759.)

Some exceptions to the number rule:

- **Be consistent in the presentation when numbers are part of a pair or series of comparable quantities** —either spell them all or write them all as numerals. Usually, numerals are more understandable. For example:

  There were 3 children in the car and 10 in the van.

  8 of 50 responses

- **Always use numerals with *percent:***

  Of the 23,823 students registered for the first semester, only 3 percent were black.

  Note: ASA style uses the word *percent* (rather than the sign) in text, including in parentheses:

  In addition, black and Hispanic drivers were more likely to report being subjected to a physical search of the driver or having their vehicles searched (black, 7.1 percent; Hispanic, 10.1 percent; and white, 2.9 percent).

- **Express numbers less than 1 million in numerals; for numbers greater than 1 million,** write a numeral followed by the word *million, billion*, and so on.

  We counted 10,500 birds.

  The population increased by 4.2 million in 1982.

- **Express numbers that represent exact time, sample sizes, and sums of money as numerals:**

  The program will run from 9:00 a.m. to 3:30 p.m.

  a $5 bill

  $N = 2,064$

2.6 Dates

The following examples illustrate dates correctly presented in text:

> nineteenth century
>
> twentieth-century poets [include a hyphen when used as an adjective]
>
> 1930s; mid-1980s
>
> January 19, 1968
>
> On January 19, 1968, the council met for the first time.
>
> April 1989 [no comma between month and year]
>
> 1928 to 1931 [in text, use *to* instead of an en dash between years]

Spell out the months in entries in a reference list and in text citations of newspaper and magazine articles (*January 19, 1968*). (See *CMOS* 2003:388–91.)

2.7 Abbreviations and Acronyms

Do not use **abbreviations** such as *etc., e.g.,* and *i.e.,* in running text. Instead, use phrases such as *and so on, for example,* or *in other words.* However, use the abbreviations in parenthetical statements.

> In other words, some terms used in specific areas of sociology (e.g., cultural capital, Blau space) are not readily understood by the general sociologist.

Use *U.S.* as an adjective, *United States* as a noun:

> U.S. currency is the medium of exchange in the United States.

Acronyms

Acronyms are terms based on the initial letters of their various elements and read as single words (*NATO, AIDS*) (*CMOS* 2003:558).

When using **acronyms,** spell out the complete term the first time it is used and present the acronym in parentheses.

First use: The Current Population Survey (CPS) includes . . .

Later: CPS data show that . . .

For examples of acronyms of terminology relating to electronic resources and publishing, see Section 5.1.

2.8 Academic Degrees

Use the following abbreviations for academic degrees (and note the capitalization of PhD and EdD):

BA (or AB)	Bachelor of Arts
BS (or SB)	Bachelor of Science
EdD	Doctor of Education
JD	Doctor of Law
LLB	Bachelor of Laws
LLD	Doctor of Laws
MA (or AM)	Master of Arts
MBA	Master of Business Administration
MD	Doctor of Medicine
MS	Master of Science
MSW	Master of Social Welfare or Master of Social Work
PhD	Doctor of Philosophy
Dphil	Doctor of Philosophy (European form)

Plurals are formed by adding an *s* (*MAs* and *PhDs*).

As a general rule, ASA recommends omitting all periods in abbreviations of academic degrees, unless they are required for tradition or consistency. See the *CMOS* (2003:563–64) for a more extensive discussion and list of abbreviations for academic degrees.

When referring to a general degree, use *master's, bachelor's,* or *doctoral degree.*

2.9 Foreign Words and Language Usage

In general, foreign words in text should be *italicized*. Commonly used foreign words or terms, however, should appear in roman type (*CMOS* 2003:291–92):

> per se, ad hoc, et al., a priori

In references, follow the same rules for titles of foreign-language publications as for English-language publications (i.e., use the headline style as described in *CMOS* 2003:367). Alterations to capitalization, however, should be done with expert help if writers and editors do not have firsthand knowledge of a foreign language.

Example of references:

> Chauí, M. 1979. *O Que é Ideologia.* São Paulo, Brazil: Brasiliense.

If translations are used, place them within parentheses immediately following the words to be translated or in brackets following a block quote (*CMOS* 2003:469–70):

> Wegener, Berndt. 1987. "Von Nutzen Entfernter Bekannter" (Benefiting from Persons We Barely Know). *Kölner Zeitschrift für Soziologie und Sozialpsychologie* 39:278–301.

Because many manuscripts are now being prepared with word processing systems that contain software with special characters (including diacritical marks and alphabetical characters that do not normally occur in English), use these characters when keyboarding foreign words. Try to maintain consistency throughout the manuscript: If special characters are used for some words, they should be used for all words that conventionally would be accented (*Québec, Montréal, Palais des Congrès de Montréal, l'Hôtel-Dieu*).

The Chicago Manual of Style (2003) includes guidelines on other aspects of foreign language usage (including use of quotations, pp. 469–71, and abbreviations, pp. 562, 565).

Chapter 10 of *CMOS* contains additional information usage on foreign languages, including the special characters that are used in a number of foreign languages.

3 ASA-Specific Usages and Conventions

The ASA Council and the Executive Office as well as committees, sections, and other entities have adopted conventions and guidelines for preferred word usages and style to be used for Association records, documents, and publications. Increasingly, ASA documents (e.g., the *ASA Code of Ethics*, Council minutes, task force and other reports, communications and public affairs releases, newsletters, research reports, programmatic records) are being widely disseminated, especially through the ASA Web site (http://www.asanet.org). The guidelines presented in this section include some of the more common ASA-specific conventions that have been adopted over the years.

3.1 Hyphenation

Hyphenate the following words when referring to officers of the ASA and when used as a title:

- Secretary-Elect

- Vice President-Elect, but Vice President

- Past-President

- President-Elect

3.2 Capitalization

Capitalize the following:

- *Sociology* only if it is part of a proper name or is used in a special context (e.g., within a title that is set in upper/lower title case)

- *Section* when speaking of a specific ASA section. Do not capitalize *section* when speaking of a section or sections in general: *Of the 42 ASA sections, the Section on Emotions . . .*

- ASA Annual Meeting, but in the aggregate ASA annual meetings

- Annual Business Meeting

- NOAH, e-NOAH

- ASA Bylaws, ASA Constitution (or references to these)

- Council (when referring to ASA Council)

- Titles of officers of the Association or official positions (the *Vice President of ASA*, *Council Liaison*)

- Title of other organization designations such as membership categories. For example, capitalize the *Emeritus Membership Category* only when referring to it specifically in this form (as a proper noun); do not capitalize it in the following: *Membership in the emeritus category increased slightly.*

- Words designating a title such as *chair, editor, editor designee*, and *legal counsel* are capitalized only when the title immediately precedes a personal name and is used as part of the name (*Chair Patricia Roos*).

- Names of ASA offices and committees (*Committee on Nominations, Chair of the Membership Committee*)

- Names of subcommittees, committees, reports, and programs. Note that later references to a specifically named entity would also be capitalized:

  Council also appointed a Subcommittee on ASA Policymaking and Resolutions, chaired by Patricia Roos. . . . In January 2000, Council asked the Subcommittee to continue its work for another year.

Do not capitalize the following:

- publications program (and other general references to procedures, policies, or programs)
- congressional, administration (*CMOS* 2003:334)
- annual meeting when referring to a non-ASA event
- section when referring to sections in general
- revised *Code of Ethics*

3.3 Italics

Italicize titles as follows:

- *Section Manual*
- *Organizers Manual*
- Annual Meeting *Program*

Do not italicize the following:

- Rose Series in Sociology
- Issues Series in Social Research and Social Policy

3.4 Preferred Word Usages

- Use *Annual Meeting* when referring to ASA's major meeting held every summer (*convention* is not acceptable).
- Use official names of committees (e.g., *Committee on Publications* is correct; *Publications Committee* or any other variant of the official name is not acceptable).
- Do not use *LISTSERV* when referring to just any electronic mailing list. *LISTSERV* is a proprietary term and should be used only when referring to the trademarked name. (See Section 5.1.)

3.5 Some ASA Style Guidelines

Titles: Do not abbreviate academic rank or title (the exception is *Dr.*).

> *Right:* Assistant Professor, Associate Professor, Professor, Vice President, President-Elect

> *Wrong:* Asst. Prof., Assoc Prof, Prof., VP, Pres. Elect

In addition, do not refer to a person's title in an article unless there is some content-specific reason for doing so (e.g., a direct quotation). Use only a person's full name or, in later references, their last name only.

Institutions: Do not abbreviate names of institutions; spell out the complete institutional name. When specifying a campus for a university, use a hyphen (Section 2.1.3).

> *Right:* University of California-Los Angeles, Rand Corporation, Louisiana State University, University of Illinois at Urbana-Champaign (Section 2.1.3)

> *Wrong:* UCLA (usually), University of California, Los Angeles, Rand Corp., LA St. U.

Addresses: For addresses in Washington, DC, there should be no comma between street and quadrant (*NW, SW, SE, NE*) and no periods in referencing quadrants or in *DC*.

> *Right:* 1430 K Street NW, Washington, DC 20005

> *Wrong:* 1430 K Street, N.W., Washington, D.C. 20005

Telephone numbers: Separate the telephone number from the address by a semicolon. Telephone numbers should always follow the style shown below, with no slash or hyphen between area code and number but always with a space between the closing area code parenthesis and the number.

> *Right:* (202) 383-9005

> *Wrong:* 202/383-9005 or 202-383-9005

State Abbreviations: Abbreviate states to the U.S. Postal Service two-letter abbreviations.

> *Right:* Miami, FL; Tupelo, MS; Denver, CO

> *Wrong:* Miami, Fla.; Tupelo, Miss.; Denver, Colo.

Numbers: When numbering a series of items within a paragraph or article, use the form *(1)*, not *1.* or *1)*.

4 Guidelines for Organizing and Presenting Content

This section provides ASA style guidelines on key elements relating to organization and presentation of content in a manuscript. Authors preparing manuscripts for publications not requiring ASA journal specifications should also see Section 4.9.

Note: Authors who are submitting a manuscript to an ASA journal: In addition to specifications set forth in this section, see Section 6.0 for required journal specification formats.

4.1 Order and Form of Required Pages

4.1.1 Title Page

A title page is recommended for all articles. This page should include the full title of the article, the name(s) and institution(s) of the author(s) (listed vertically if more than one), a running head, the word count for the manuscript (including footnotes and references), and a title footnote. An asterisk (*) following the title refers to the title footnote at the bottom of the title page. This footnote includes the name and address of the corresponding author, acknowledgments, credits, and grant numbers.

For an example of a title page, see Section 6.1.2.

4.1.2 Abstract

The abstract begins on a separate page following the title page, with the title repeated as a heading. Omit author identification. The abstract should be a brief (no more than 200 words) and descriptive summary of the most important contributions of a paper. Restrict the abstract to one paragraph.

4.1.3 Text

Begin the text of a manuscript on a new page headed by the manuscript title. Omit author identification throughout the text. Include the footnotes, appendices, tables, and figures in separate sections following the text. Figure captions are left-justified below the figure, while table titles are left-justified above the table.

4.2 Subheadings

Subheadings should clearly indicate the organization of the content of the manuscript. Generally, three heading levels are sufficient for a full-length article. Some general guidelines follow:

THIS IS A FIRST-LEVEL HEAD

First-level heads are in all caps, left-justified. Some ASA journals do not indent the paragraph immediately following a first-level head. The beginning of a manuscript should not have a heading (i.e., do not begin with the heading *Introduction*).

This Is a Second-Level Head

Second-level heads are in italics and left-justified. Capitalize all words except prepositions (*of, into, between, through*), articles (*a, an, the*), and coordinating conjunctions (*and, but, or*). Some ASA journals do not indent the paragraph immediately following a second-level head.

 This is a third-level head.

Third-level heads are run-in heads, in italics, indented at the beginning of the paragraph, and followed by a period. The paragraph continues immediately after the period. Capitalize only the first letter and proper nouns in a third-level head.

4.3 Text Citations, References, and Bibliographies

The *ASA Style Guide* follows the author-date system of citation in *The Chicago Manual of Style* (2003:616–24), which includes a brief text citation (enclosed in parentheses) and a complete list of references cited (included at the end of an article, before any appendices).

Although ASA journals use only the text citations/reference system for cited works in an article, under certain circumstances authors may need to prepare a bibliography (e.g., when preparing a book-length manuscript). Bibliographies are similar (but not identical) to reference lists (in general, in addition to works cited they may also include other relevant sources) (see *CMOS* 2003:612–16).

4.3.1 Text Citations

Citations in the text include the last name of the author(s) and year of publication. Include page numbers when quoting directly from a work or referring to specific passages. Identify subsequent citations of the same source in the same way as the first. Examples follow:

- If the **author's name is in the text,** follow it with the publication year in parentheses:

  . . . in another study by Duncan (1959).

- If the **author's name is not in the text,** enclose the last name and publication year in parentheses:

  . . . whenever it occurred (Gouldner 1963).

- **Pagination** follows the year of publication after a colon, with no space between the colon and the page number:

  . . . Kuhn (1970:71).

  Note: This is the preferred ASA style. Older forms of text citations are not acceptable: (Kuhn 1970, p. 71).

- Give both last names for **joint authors:**

  . . . (Martin and Bailey 1988).

- If a work has **three authors**, cite all three last names in the first citation in the text; thereafter, use *et al.* in the citation. If a work has **more than three authors**, use *et al.* in the first citation and in all subsequent citations.

  First citation for a work with three authors: . . . had been lost (Carr, Smith, and Jones 1962).

  Later: . . . (Carr et al. 1962)

- If a work cited was reprinted from a **version published earlier**, list the earliest publication date in brackets, followed by the publication date of the recent version used:

  . . . Veblen ([1899] 1979) stated that . . .

- **Separate a series of references with semicolons.** List the series in alphabetical or date order, but be consistent throughout the manuscript.

  . . . (Green 1995; Mundi 1987; Smith and Wallop 1989).

- For **unpublished materials**, use *forthcoming* to indicate material scheduled for publication. For dissertations and unpublished papers, cite the date. If no date is available, use *N.d.* (no date) in place of the date:

  Previous studies by Smith (forthcoming) and Jones (N.d.) concluded . . .

- For **National Archives or other archival sources**, use abbreviated citations in the text:

  . . . (NA, RG 381, Box 780, April 28, 1965; Meany Archives, LRF, Box 6, March 18, 1970).

- For **machine-readable data files**, cite authorship and date:

  . . . (Institute for Survey Research 1976).

- Text citations for **e-resources** generally follow the preceding guidelines; for specific information, see Section 5.3.

4.3.2 Reference Lists

A reference list follows the text and footnotes in a separate section headed *References*. All references cited in the text must be listed in the reference section, and vice versa. It is the author's responsibility to ensure that publication information for each entry is complete and correct. ASA journal editors will check the format of a reference list but will not check the accuracy of titles or the spelling of names. Authors should thus **double-check** the details.

Like all other parts of a manuscript, the references should be **double-spaced**.

(Also see the Appendix for examples.)

The Basic Forms for ASA References

Most sources cited in ASA journals and publications come from books and periodicals, either in a printed format or in the electronic version (or both). The examples that follow demonstrate the most common usages.

Books

Author1 (last name inverted), **Author2** (including full surname, last name is not inverted)**, and Author3. Year of publication. *Name of Publication (italicized).* **Location of publisher, state, or province postal code** (or name of country if a foreign publisher)**: Publisher's Name.**

Note: For all types of references, when there are only two authors or editors, there is no comma after the name of the first author or editor.

Bursik, Robert J., Jr. and Harold G. Grasmick. 1993. *Neighborhoods and Crime: The Dimensions of Effective Community Control.* New York: Lexington Books.

Hagan, John and Ruth D. Peterson, eds. 1995. *Crime and Inequality.* Stanford, CA: Stanford University Press.

Jaynes, Gerald D. and Robin M. Williams, Jr. 1989. *A Common Destiny: Blacks and American Society.* Washington, DC: National Academy Press.

Note: Only the Bursik and Grasmick reference has no state location for publisher (see guidelines below).

Journal Articles

Author1 (last name inverted)**, Author2** (including full surname, last name is not inverted)**, and Author3. Year of publication. "Title of Article."** *Name of Publication (italicized)* **Volume Number(Issue Number):page numbers of article.**

Aseltine, Robert H., Jr. and Ronald C. Kessler. 1993. "Marital Disruption and Depression in a Community Sample." *Journal of Health and Social Behavior* 34(3):237–51.

Gans, Herbert J. 2005. "Race as Class." *Contexts* 4(4):17–21.

Kalleberg, Arne L., Barbara F. Reskin, and Ken Hudson. 2000. "Bad Jobs in America: Standard and Non-standard Employment Relations and Job Quality in the United States." *American Sociological Review* 65(2):256–78.

Logan, John R. 2005. "Re-Placing Whiteness: Where's the Beef?" *City & Community* 4(2):137–42.

Moen, Phyllis, Jungmeen E. Kim, and Heather Hofmeister. 2001. "Couples' Work/Retirement Transitions, Gender, and Marital Quality." *Social Psychology Quarterly* 64(1):55–75.

Note: The preceding examples include the issue number after the volume number of the journal. In a departure from the second edition, the *ASA Style Guide* now suggests that issue numbers be included as well. If issue numbers are used, they should be used throughout the reference list.

ASA allows editorial discretion in changing *&* to *and* in book and journal titles, but recommends retaining *&* if it is part of a trademarked title.

Chapters in Books or Other Collected Works

Author1 (last name inverted)**, Author2** (including full surname, last name is not inverted)**, and Author3. Year of publication. "Title of article." Pp.** (with page numbers, elided) **in *Name of Publication (italicized)*, edited by Editor1, Editor2, and Editor3** (editors' initials only for first/middle names, names not inverted)**. Location of publisher, state, or province postal code** (or name of country if a foreign publisher)**: Publisher's Name.**

McAdam, Doug and Kelly Moore. 1989. "The Politics of Black Insurgency, 1930–1975." Pp. 255–85 in *Violence in America*. Vol. 2, *Protest, Rebellion, Reform*, edited by T. R. Gurr. Newbury Park, CA: Sage Publications.

Riley, Matilda White. 1985. "Women, Men, and the Lengthening Life Course." Pp. 333–47 in *Gender and the Life Course*, edited by A. S. Rossi. New York: Aldine.

Zatz, Marjorie S. and Richard P. Krecker, Jr. 2003. "Antigang Initiatives as Racialized Policy." Pp. 173–96 in *Crime Control and Social Justice: The Delicate Balance*, edited by D. F. Hawkins, S. L. Myers, Jr., and R. N. Stone. Westport, CT: Greenwood Press.

Note: In the McAdam and Moore reference, the form of the volume number is a change in this third edition of the *ASA Style Guide.*

Articles from E-Resources

Articles and books obtained from the Internet follow the same pattern as those cited above, with the exception that page numbers are omitted and the URL and date of access are included.

> Schafer, Daniel W. and Fred L. Ramsey. 2003. "Teaching the Craft of Data Analysis." *Journal of Statistics Education* 11(1). Retrieved December 12, 2006 (http://www.amstat.org/publications/jse/v11n1/schafer.html).

> Thomas, Jan E., ed. 2005. *Incorporating the Women Founders into Classical Theory Courses.* Washington, DC: American Sociological Association. Retrieved December 12, 2006 (http://www.enoah.net/ASA/ASAShopOnlineService/ProductDetails.aspx?productID=ASAOE378T05E).

Section 5 contains more detailed information on the use of e-resources.

See the Appendix for examples of how to cite other types of documents (e.g., unpublished papers, presentations, magazines, newspapers, and archival sources).

Additional Guidelines

- List all references in **alphabetical order** by first authors' last names.

- Include **first names** and **surnames** for all authors. Use first-name initials only if an author used initials in the original publication. In these cases, add a space between the initials, as in *R. B. Brown* and *M. L. B. Smith.*

- Do not use the ampersand (*&*) for *and* in joining names.

- For **multiple authorship,** invert only the first author's name (*Jones, Arthur B., Colin D. Smith, and James Petersen*). List all authors. Using *et al.* in the reference section is not acceptable unless a work was authored by a committee. Do not place a comma between two names, but place commas between three or more names.

- For **two or more listings under the same author(s) or editor(s),** list them in the order of year of publication, earliest year first. For repeated authors or editors, use six hyphens and a period (------.) or three em dashes and a period (———.) in place of the name(s).

- Distinguish works by the **same author(s) in the same year** by adding letters (*1982a, 1982b, 1982c*). List such works in alphabetical order by title. Edited works by the same author are listed with original works.

    Fyfe, James J. 1982a. "Blind Justice: Police Shootings in Memphis." *The Journal of Criminal Law and Criminology* 73(2):707–22.

    ———. 1982b. "Race and Extreme Police-Citizen Violence." Pp.173–94 in *Readings on Police Use of Deadly Force*, edited by J. J. Fyfe. New York: Police Foundation.

- If **no date** is available, use *N.d.* in place of the date. If the cited material is unpublished but has been accepted for publication, use *Forthcoming* in place of the date and give the name of the publisher or journal.

- With the exception of New York, include both the **city and state** for the place of publication. Use the **U.S. Postal Code abbreviations** for states in a reference list (*WI; NY; Washington, DC*). *The Chicago Manual of*

Style (2003:566–567) provides a complete list of U.S. and Canadian geographic terms. For foreign cities, also provide the name of the country.

- For **dissertations, unpublished papers, and presented papers,** cite the date and location where the paper was presented or is available.

- The **form of citing volume number** in collected works has changed in the third edition of the *ASA Style Guide*. (The form is consistent with citing book volumes generally.)

> Clausen, John A. 1972. "The Life Course of Individuals." Pp. 457–514 in *Aging and Society*. Vol. 3, *A Sociology of Age Stratification*, edited by M. W. Riley, M. Johnson, and A. Foner. New York: Russell Sage.

4.4 Legal Citations and Government Documents

This section provides some guidelines for citing the more common sources from executive, legislative, and judicial proceedings. The rules are adapted from *The Chicago Manual of Style* and *The Bluebook: A Uniform System of Citation*, 17th ed. (2000). *The Bluebook* is published by the Harvard Law Review Association and is the most widely used style guide for legal citations.

The guidelines are adapted for nonlegal works. In general, the ASA style recommends that (1) all references, including those from legal periodicals, should be included in a reference list (rather than in footnotes, as is the case in legal periodicals); and (2) consistency should be maintained in citing legal references. Authors may need to use discretion in determining how to create text citations and references for legal citations (e.g., use of abbreviations, when citations should appear in running text, and when references are appropriate). As with other cited source material, references to legal sources should provide complete and accurate information so that a reader can locate the information easily.

The following are some of the more commonly used abbreviations referring to court, public law, and other legal citations (they are not italicized):

U.S.C.	United States Code
U.S.	U.S. Reports
F.	Federal Reporter
F.2d	Federal Reporter, 2nd Series
F. Supp.	Federal Supplement
C.F.R.	Code of Federal Regulations.
H.R.	U.S. House of Representatives
S.	U.S. Senate

Terms such as *Congress, Session, Congressional Record, Federal Register,* and *U.S. Statutes-at-Large* are not abbreviated.

These guidelines cover only a small number of examples from the large array of law-related sources. Many of the sources referred to below are now available online (both current and historical)—through the THOMAS feature of the Library of Congress (http://thomas.loc.gov) or subscription databases such as LexisNexis.

4.4.1 Legal Citations

In nonlegal works, legal citations are generally entered in running text with additional information (if necessary) in footnotes or endnotes. References to constitutions, executive orders or amicus briefs, for example, would not require a reference:

> The American Sociological Association filed an amicus brief in *Grutter v. Bollinger* (539 U.S. 306 [2003]) . . .

> Executive Order 11246 established the Office for Federal Contract Compliance . . .

Legal citations, however, may also be included in text citations and reference lists, especially for court decisions, statutes, and certain types of legislative materials.

- **Reference to constitutions, laws, ordinances:**

  U.S. Constitution: U.S. Constitution, Article 1, Section 4.

  State constitutions: Arkansas Constitution, Article 7, Section 5.

  Public law: *Telecommunications Act of 1996*, Public Law 104–104, 110 U.S. Statutes at Large 56 (1996).

  U.S. Code: *Declaratory Judgment Act*, 28 U.S.C. 2201 (1952).

  State Law: Ohio Revised Code Annotated, Section 3566 (West 2000).

- **Reference to court decisions:** If cases are retrieved from an online database (e.g., LexisNexis or HeinOnline), access information should be included. *Note:* Case names (including "v.") are italicized:

  U.S. Supreme Court: *Brown v. Board of Education*, 347 U.S. 483 (1954).

  Lower federal courts: *Black Firefighters Association of Dallas v. City of Dallas*, 19 F.3d 992 (1994).

  Lower federal courts: *Quirin v. City of Pittsburgh* 1992, 801 F. Supp. 1486 (1992).

  State courts: *Williams v. Davis*, 27 Cal. 2d 746 (1946).

  State courts: *Ohio v. Vincer* (Ohio App. Lexis 4356 [1999]).

- **Reference to legal periodicals and treatises:** In general follow the rules for citing books and periodicals specified in Section 4.3:

    Text: (Butler 1996)

    Reference:
    Butler, Paul. 1996. "Affirmative Action and the Criminal Law." *University of Colorado Law Review* 68(4):841–89.

Note also that the *ASA Style Guide* calls for italicizing cases in titles, even when not italicized in the published article.

    Text: (Baldus et al. 1998)

    Reference:
    Baldus, David C., George Woodworth, David Zuckerman, Neil Alan Weiner, and Barbara Broffitt. 1998. "Racial Discrimination and the Death Penalty in the Post-*Furman* Era: An Empirical and Legal Overview, with Recent Findings from Philadelphia." *Cornell Law Review* 83(6):1638–770.

4.4.2 Public Documents in General

This section provides guidelines for commonly cited documents and materials issued by government institutions and agencies in the United States.

For text citations: For institutional or government authorship, supply minimum identification from the beginning of the complete citation.

    . . . (U.S. Bureau of the Census 1963:117).

For references:

- **If names of authors, editors, or compilers are provided, use the following method:**

    Bonczar, Thomas P. and Allen J. Beck. 1997. *Lifetime Likelihood of Going to State or Federal Prison.* Bureau of

Justice Statistics Special Bulletin, NCJ 160092. Washington, DC: U.S. Department of Justice.

- **If names of author(s), editor(s), or compiler(s) are not provided, include some or all of the following in references to printed public documents:**
    - Country, state, city, or other government agency that issued the document
    - Legislative body, executive department, court bureau, committee, etc.
    - Divisions, regional offices, etc.
    - Date
    - Title of the document
    - Name of series or collection
    - Report number [if included]
    - Publisher
    - Page number(s) [if relevant]

- **Example references from executive department agencies:**

    U.S. Department of Justice. Bureau of Justice Statistics. 1984. *Criminal Victimization in the U.S., 1983*. Washington, DC: U.S. Government Printing Office.

    U.S. Bureau of the Census. 1960. *Characteristics of Population*. Vol. 1. Washington, DC: U.S. Government Printing Office.

    Note: Cite publications of the Bureau of Census either as *U.S. Department of Commerce. Bureau of the Census* or as *U.S. Bureau of the Census*. (See *CMOS* 2003:742.)

- **Example references from congressional sources:** Some information (e.g., bills, resolutions, committee activity, and the *Congressional Record*) are available online through the THOMAS feature of the Library of Congress (http://thomas.loc.gov). (However, ensure that links to the Web sites work.)

Debates:

> U.S. Congress. House of Representatives. 1995. *Violent Criminal Incarceration Act of 1995.* H.R. 667, 104th Congress, 1st Session. Congressional Record 141 (February 9, 1995):H1479.

Bills:

> U.S. Congress. House of Representatives. *Fair Minimum Wage Act of 2007.* H.R. 2. 110th Congress, 1st Session, 2007. Retrieved January 13, 2007 (http://thomas.loc.gov).

Hearings:

> U.S. Congress. Senate. 1992. *Hate Crimes Statistics Act: Hearing before the Subcommittee on the Constitution of the Committee on the Judiciary.* 102nd Congress, 2nd Session, August 5, 1992.

Report:

> U.S. Congress. Senate. Committee on Health, Education, Labor, and Pensions. 2006. *Combating Autism Act of 2005.* Committee Report. 109th Congress, 2nd Session. Retrieved January 12, 2007 (http://frwebgate.access.gpo.gov/cgi-bin/getdoc.cgi?dbname=109_cong_reports&docid=f:sr318.109.pdf).

(See Sections 6 and 12 in the Appendix for additional examples.)

4.5 Footnotes and Endnotes

Footnotes should be indicated in the text by consecutive superscripted Arabic numerals. To refer to a footnote again later in the text, use a parenthetical note, such as *(See note 3)*.

Footnotes or endnotes can (1) explain or amplify text, (2) cite materials of limited availability, or (3) be added to a table to present additional information.

Use footnotes and endnotes only when necessary. Notes (particularly long ones) can be distracting to the reader. As alternatives, consider incorporating information in footnotes into text, stating in the text (for example) that the information is available from the author or adding an appendix.

Type **footnotes** in numerical order, **double-spaced** at the bottom of the manuscript page or in a separate section titled *Notes* or *Endnotes.* Begin each footnote with the superscript Arabic numeral to which it is keyed in the text.

[9]After 1981 there was . . .

4.6 Appendices

If only one appendix is included, refer to it as *Appendix.* For example, the title might read:

Appendix. Variable Names and Definitions

If more than one appendix is included, each should be lettered (to distinguish it from numbered figures and tables in the text). For example, the title might read:

Appendix A. Variable Names and Definitions

Appendix B. Questions Included in the Survey

4.7 Mathematical Symbols and Equations

Important equations discussed in the text should be identified by consecutive Arabic numbers in parentheses at the right-hand margin. Clarify all unusual characters or symbols with notes circled in the margin. Use *italic* type for variables and ***bold italic*** type for vectors or matrices.

4.8 Tables, Figures, and Graphic Materials

4.8.1 Tables

The following conventions and examples provide general guidelines on presentation of tables:

- **Number** tables consecutively throughout the text, and type or print each table on a separate sheet at the end of the manuscript. Insert a note in the text to indicate the approximate placement of each table (e.g., *TABLE 2 ABOUT HERE*).

- Include a **descriptive title** for each table. Specify what the table presents (means, coefficients, percentages) and include information about the dataset and time frame. Include who/what, when, and where in table (and figure) titles to provide an accurate and comprehensive description (particularly important if the table is ever viewed independently of the accompanying article).

- Include **headings** for all columns and rows. Avoid abbreviations in columns and row headings. Spell out *percent* in headings. Use subheadings to separate different sections of the tables or to clarify categories of variables.

- Take measurement techniques into consideration when determining the best way to present the data (i.e., how many decimal places make sense). In general, carry out decimal fractions to the thousandths place and omit leading zeros (i.e., *.372* instead of *0.372*).

Standard errors, *t*-statistics, and so on may appear in parentheses under the coefficients with an explanatory note identifying these statistics for the reader (see example below). Alternatively, they may be presented in a separate column.

Gather general notes to a table as *Notes* or *Sources* beneath the table. Use *a, b, c*, and so on to add explanatory **footnotes** to the table. List full citations of the data sources in the references.

Use **asterisks** *, **, and *** to indicate statistical significance at the .05, .01, and .001 levels, respectively. Specify one-tailed or two-tailed tests. Generally, results not significant at the $p < .05$ level or better (such as $p < .10$) should not be indicated in tables or discussed in text as significant. Tables that present variables with different metrics are problematic because values may require different numerical formats and interpretations. The tables shown below provide illustrations:

Table 4. OLS Coefficients from the Multiple Linear Regression of Monthly Earnings on Selected Independent Variables, Urban China, 1996: Three-Worker-Type Analysis

Variable	Restrictive Measure		Broad Measure		Comprehensive Measure	
	Model 4a	Model 5a	Model 4b	Model 5b	Model 4c	Model 5c
Education (years of schooling)	.049*** (.009)	.045*** (.010)	.053*** (.008)	.045*** (.009)	.057*** (.007)	.047*** (.006)
Experience	.010** (.005)	.009* (.005)	.010* (.004)	.008 (.005)	.014*** (.004)	.013*** (.004)
(Experience)^2 × 1,000	−.153* (.074)	−.144* (.070)	−.160* (.074)	−.099 (.070)	−.203** (.071)	-0.167** (.060)
Party member (yes = 1)	.121** (.038)	.126** (.037)	.138*** (.035)	.145*** (.035)	.142*** (.037)	.149*** (.037)
Sex (male = 1)	.218*** (.040)	.213*** (.040)	.220*** (.038)	.210*** (.039)	.225*** (.038)	.216*** (.038)
Later entrants[a]	.312* (.144)	−.732 (.370)	.238*** (.068)	−.263 (.193)	.313*** (.071)	−.175 (.182)
Early birds	.553 (.439)	.130 (.602)	.184 (.230)	−.124 (.266)	.151 (.206)	−.067 (.249)
Later entrants × Education	—	.122* (.047)	—	.060* (.022)	—	.056** (.019)
Early birds × Education	—	.051 (.103)	—	.037 (.031)	—	.025 (.024)
Constant	5.305*** (.156)	5.348*** (.165)	5.238*** (.140)	5.333*** (.153)	5.124*** (.106)	5.230*** (.116)
Number of cases	2,072		2,061		2,060	
R^2	.117	.129	.114	.123	.127	.136

Notes: Numbers in parentheses are standard errors adjusted for clustering on counties. Data are weighted.
[a] "Stayers" is the reference category; market losers are omitted from the analysis because of the small number of cases (N = 19).
*$p < .05$ **$p < .01$ ***$p < .001$ (two-tailed tests)

Table 1. Means (or Proportions) and Standard Deviations (in Parentheses) of the Variables Used in the Analysis, by Gender

Variable	Males N = 1,323	Females N = 1,427	Mean Difference p Values
Current Aggression	.30 (.45)	.21 (.40)	.000
Role Stress	.54 (1.02)	.72 (1.19)	.000
Adolescent Aggression	.43 (.49)	.24 (.43)	.000
Depressive Symptoms (Adolescent)	3.01 (2.57)	3.30 (2.50)	.002
Illicit Drug Use (Adolescent)	.05 (.22)	.04 (.20)	.226
Delinquent Peers (Adolescent)	.47 (.86)	.46 (.88)	.701
Deviant Attitudes (Adolescent)	1.79 (1.48)	1.45 (1.38)	.000
Conventional Attachment (Adolescent)	2.77 (1.13)	3.01 (1.16)	.000
Lack of Self-control (Adolescent)	1.72 (1.16)	1.20 (1.02)	.000
Level of Education	7.87 (1.41)	7.93 (1.37)	.257
Marital Status	.50 (.50)	.62 (.48)	.000
Parental Status	.25 (.43)	.37 (.48)	.000
Interview Year	3.30 (2.28)	3.24 (2.23)	.465

4.8.2 Figures

Visual art—figures, illustrations, and photographs—are published in ASA journals only when they add unquestionably to a reader's understanding of the research being presented. In general, before including figures in a manuscript, consider objectively the importance of the visual presentations to be included. The figure shown below provides an illustration:

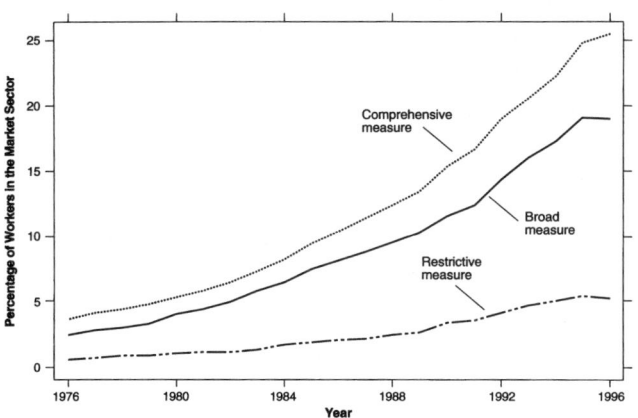

Figure 2. Percentages of Urban Workers in China's Market Sector, 1976 to 1996: A Comparison of Three Measures

Number figures, illustrations, or photographs consecutively throughout the manuscript. Each should include a title. Insert a note in the text to indicate approximate placement (e.g., *FIGURE 1 ABOUT HERE*). Send printouts or photocopies of figures, illustrations, and photographs when submitting the manuscript. If the manuscript is accepted for publication, however, photographs and art must be submitted in camera-ready form. (Some ASA journals will request artwork as an electronic file if it is available. See Section 6.5 for text and graphic file formats accepted by some ASA journals.)

4.8.3 Illustrations and Photographs

Camera-ready **illustrations** and **figures** must be executed by computer or by a graphic artist in black ink on white paper with clear lines. All lettering on figures and illustrations must be typeset. **Photographs** must be black and white on glossy paper.

Important: *All artwork and type must be legible when reduced to fit one or two column widths, 2-9/16 inches wide and 5-5/16 inches wide, respectively.*

Author(s) must secure permission to publish any copyrighted figure, illustration, or photograph before it can appear in any ASA journal.

4.9 General Manuscript Formats and Style (Non-ASA Journals)

The *ASA Style Guide* is primarily intended to guide authors who are submitting manuscripts to ASA journals. However, because the ASA style has been used widely in many other venues (e.g., preparation of sociological theses, dissertations, and oral presentations, and in publishing on topics in other social science fields), this section includes a few basic guidelines on factors authors should consider when preparing manuscripts for publications other than ASA journals.

Users of this *Style Guide* are advised to consult with their departments, agencies, organizations, or publishers on specific requirements for issues such as the following:

- Page format requirements, including keyboarding instructions (e.g., margins, preferred font, indentation of paragraphs, spacing).

- The nature, format, content, and order of required pages (e.g., title pages, acknowledgments, abstracts, references, appendices, tables, figures).

- Mechanics of style (e.g., special rules on punctuation and capitalization).

- Style requirements relating to headings, text citations and references, mathematical expressions, tables and figures, and other supporting materials.

- Requirements and procedures for transmission of manuscripts to departments or publishers (for example), including transmission in electronic formats.

Although the three checklists presented in Section 6.6 are directed specifically to requirements of ASA journals, they offer some ideas for standards relating to mechanics and style that might apply to manuscripts more generally.

5 Guidelines for Using Electronic Resources (E-Resources)

Publishing environments have changed dramatically over the past decade, particularly relating to the Internet and to electronic forms of presentation in general. Although source material on the Internet presents new challenges for documentation in writing and research (for example, the meaning, nature, and form of electronic resources are still evolving), some basic guidelines for standards have emerged. The direction provided here is based on *The Chicago Manual of Style* (2003) for referring to or citing the most common types of e-resources currently used by social scientists in research and writing.

The Chicago Manual of Style online (http://www.chicago-manualofsstyle.org/tools_citationguide.html) also provides a useful quick guide to citations, which includes examples of the most common types of electronic references.

(A review of style guides used by other professional and scientific associations also provided valuable insights in defining issues and setting some ground rules for this *ASA Style Guide*.)

In general, information about three types of e-resources will be covered:

- **Journal articles, periodicals, reports, and books** (or parts of them), which are now widely available through the Internet. Some of these exist only in online forms, but many other online periodicals in fact replicate their printed versions (and they are not likely to change in form). Examples include journal articles available through JSTOR and a report or bulletin in PDF form on the Bureau of Justice Statistics (BJS) Web site.

- **Other sources available on the Internet,** such as Web sites, periodicals, zines, Web logs (or "blogs"), electronic mailing lists, documents, records, data, codekeys, and Web-based newsletters.

- **Publications, documents, and data available in various formats** such as Machine Readable Data Files (MRDF), CD-ROM, DVD, videocassettes, and other media forms.

5.1 Some Key Terms and Definitions for Electronic Resources

The list below includes preferred spelling and definitions for some key terms used for electronic resources. The forms of the acronyms (including capitalization and hyphenation) and definitions are drawn from several sources, including *The Chicago Manual of Style* (2003:211, 823–40), homepages, and Webopedia (http://www.webopedia.com), a free online dictionary for words, phrases, and abbreviations that are related to computer and Internet technology.

In determining when words should be hyphenated (*e-mail, e-commerce*): For compound expressions that include "electronic" (*electronic-commerce, electronic-loan, electronic-mail*), abbreviate "electronic" and hyphenate words according to the form of *e-commerce, e-loan, e-journal,* and *e-mail.*

In the following list, an asterisk (*) indicates that all three forms are acceptable.

ASCII
American Standard Code for Information Interchange. ASCII codes only letters, numerals, punctuation marks, spaces, returns, line feeds, and tabs with no additional formatting. Text files are often referred to as ASCII files, although other kinds of data (such as SGML and PostScript) can also be stored as ASCII files. (*CMOS*)

Attachment
A file attached to an e-mail message. Many e-mail systems only support sending text files as e-mail. If the attachment is a binary file or formatted text file (such as an MS Word document), it must be encoded before it is sent and decoded once it is received. There are a number of encoding schemes, the two most prevalent being Uuencode and MIME. Retrieved January 15, 2007 (http://www.webopedia.com/TERM/a/attachment.html).

Beta testing
The final checking of a computer application (such as a Web site) before it is released. (*CMOS*)

Bitmap
A digital representation of an image consisting of an array of pixels, in rows and columns that can be saved to a file. (*CMOS*)

Blog
(n.) Short for Web log, a blog is a Web page that serves as a publicly accessible personal journal for an individual. Typically updated daily, blogs often reflect the personality of the author. (v.) To author a Web log. Other forms: Blogger (a person who blogs). Retrieved January 15, 2007 (http://www.webopedia.com/TERM/b/blog.html).

Breadcrumbs
A Web site navigation technique that typically appears horizontally near the top of a Web page, providing links back to each previous page that the user navigates through in order to get to the current page. Basically, breadcrumbs provide a trail for the user to follow back to the starting/entry point of a Web site and may look something like this:

home page > section page > sub section page

This technique also is referred to as a breadcrumb trail. Retrieved January 15, 2007 (http://www.webopedia.com/TERM/b/bread_crumbs.html).

CD-ROM
Compact disc read-only memory. A type of compact disc used for storing digital data that can be read optically and processed by a computer. (*CMOS*)

CRC
Camera-ready copy. Artwork and text that are ready to be photographed for reproduction without further alteration. (*CMOS*)

Database
A collection of information organized in such a way that a computer program can quickly select desired pieces of data. Retrieved January 15, 2007 (http://www.webopedia.com/TERM/d/database.html).

Digital
Transmitted or stored in an electronic format consisting of a sequence of discrete bits (0s and 1s), as with data such as text and images. (*CMOS*)

Disk, disc
Disk is the usual spelling (floppy disk). *Disc* is preferred in a few specialized applications (compact disc). (*CMOS:* 2003:211)

DOI
Digital Object Identifier. A means of identifying a piece of intellectual property on a digital network and associating it with related current data in a structured extensible way. A DOI differs from a URL because it defines an object as a first-entity, not simply the place where the object is located. Retrieved January 12, 2007 (http://www.doi.org/faq.html).

Dpi
Dots per inch. A measurement of the resolution of a printed image. The term is also used to describe the maximum resolution of the output device (as in a 1200-dpi printer). (*CMOS*)

DTD
Document type definition. In SGML or XML, a set of rules about the structure of a document that dictate the relationship among different tags and allowable text or elements within specified tags. (*CMOS*)

DVD
Digital versatile (or video) disc. A type of compact disc that can store up to 17 gigabytes of digital video, audio, or computer data. (*CMOS*)

E-commerce
Electronic commerce. Business that is conducted over the Internet using any of the applications that rely on the Internet, such as e-mail, instant messaging, shopping carts, and Web services such as FTP among others. Electronic commerce can be between two businesses transmitting funds, goods, services and/or data or between a business and a customer. Retrieved January 15, 2007 (http://www.webopedia.com/TERM/e/electronic_commerce.html).

E-mail
Electronic mail. The transmission of messages over communications networks. Retrieved January 15, 2007 (http://www.webopedia.com/TERM/e/e_mail.html).

E-NOAH
A dedicated association database and management software system developed and licensed by JL Systems of Annandale, VA. (ASA membership data are built on e-NOAH.)

EPS, eps, .eps*
Encapsulated PostScript file. A type of file used to encode graphics so they can be embedded in a larger PostScript file. (*CMOS*)

File
A block of digital information with a unique name and location in a computer system or external storage medium (such as a disk) that can be accessed and manipulated by users of the system or by the system itself. Programs, documents, and images are all examples of data stored in files. (*CMOS*)

FTP
File transfer protocol. The protocol, or set of instructions and syntax, for moving files between computers on the Internet. (*CMOS*)

GIF, gif, .gif*
Pronounced jiff or giff (hard g). *Graphics interchange format.* A
bit-mapped graphics file format used by the World Wide Web,
CompuServe, and many Bulletin Board Systems. GIF supports
color and various resolutions. It also includes data compression,
but because it is limited to 256 colors, it is more effective for
scanned images such as illustrations rather than color photos.
Retrieved January 15, 2007 (http://www.webopedia.com/TERM/
G/GIF.html).

Homepage
The main page of a Web site. Typically, the homepage serves as an
index or table of contents to other documents stored at the site.
Retrieved January 15, 2007 (http://www.webopedia.com/TERM/
h/home_page.html).

Host
A computer system that is accessed by a user working at a remote
location. Typically, the term is used when there are two computer
systems connected by modems and telephone lines. The system
that contains the data is called the host, while the computer at
which the user sits is called the remote terminal. Retrieved January 15, 2007 (http://www.webopedia.com/TERM/h/host.html).

HTML, html, .html*
HyperText Markup Language. A specific set of tags used to describe
the structure of hypertext documents that make up most Web
pages. Web browsers interpret these tags to display the text and
graphics on a Web page. HTML is an application of SGML.
(*CMOS*)

Hypertext
The organization of digital information into associations connected by links. In a hypertext environment, objects such as text
and images can contain links to other objects in the same file or in
external files, which users can choose to follow. (*CMOS*)

Internet
A global, public network of computers and computer networks
that communicate using TCP/IP (Transmission Control Protocol/

Internet Protocol). The Internet is used for such applications as e-mail and the World Wide Web. (*CMOS*)

JPEG, jpeg, .jpg*
Joint Photographic Experts Group. Pronounced jay-peg. JPEG is a lossy compression technique for color images. (Lossy compression techniques attempt to eliminate redundant or unnecessary information, resulting in some loss of data.) Although it can reduce files sizes to about 5 percent of their normal size, some detail is lost in the compression. Retrieved January 15, 2007 (http://www. webopedia.com/TERM/J/JPEG.html).

JSTOR
Journal Storage: The Scholarly Journal Archive. JSTOR is a not-for-profit organization with a dual mission to create and maintain a trusted archive of important scholarly journals and to provide access to these journals as widely as possible. JSTOR offers researchers the ability to retrieve high-resolution, scanned images of journal issues and pages as they were originally designed, printed, and illustrated. The journals archived in JSTOR span many disciplines. Retrieved January 14, 2007 (http://www.jstor. org/about/desc.html).

LISTSERV
Trademarked, proprietary name, which has been widely used as a generic term for "electronic mailing list." LISTSERV should only be used when it is clear that the trademarked version is being referenced. Retrieved January 15, 2007 (http://www.webopedia. com/TERM/L/Listserv.html).

OCR
Optical character recognition. A technology that converts images of text into character data that can be manipulated like any other digital text. (*CMOS*)

Online
Connected to, served by, or available through a system and especially a computer or telecommunications system (as the Internet). Retrieved January 14, 2007 (http://www.m-w.com/dictionary/on-line).

PDF, pdf, .pdf*

Portable Document Format. An Adobe file format to which a
PostScript file can be converted without loss of fonts, formatting, or graphics. This format is preferable to PostScript in certain
situations because it allows some editing, compresses the amount
of memory needed for the graphics, and is more uniform, causing
fewer problems at the printer. (*CMOS*)

Pixel

The basic unit that constitutes a digital image. Each pixel contains
black and white, grayscale, or color information about the square
it represents. (*CMOS*)

Protocol

An agreed-upon format for transmitting data between two
devices. The protocol determines the following: the type of error
checking to be used; data compression method, if any; how the
sending device will indicate that it has finished sending a message;
and how the receiving device will indicate that it has received a
message. There are a variety of standard protocols from which
programmers can choose. Retrieved January 15, 2007 (http://
www.webopedia.com/TERM/p/protocol.html).

Resolution

The number of pixels per unit of measure used to form an image.
In the United States, image resolution is calculated per inch: the
more pixels per inch, the higher the quality of the image. (*CMOS*)

Scan

To produce a digital bitmap of an image (text or graphics) using
a device that senses alternating patterns of light and dark and of
color. The resolution and scaling percentage of the desired output
should be considered before the image is scanned. (*CMOS*)

Search engines

A program that searches documents for specified keywords and
returns a list of the documents where the keywords were found.
Although search engine is really a general class of programs, the
term is often used to specifically describe systems like Alta Vista
that enable users to search for documents on the World Wide

Web and USENET newsgroups. Retrieved February 28, 2007 (http://www.webopedia.com/TERM/s/search_engine.html).

SGML
Standard Generalized Markup Language. An international standard for constructing sets of tags. SGML is not a specific set of tags but a system for defining vocabularies of tags (the names of the tags and what they mean) and using them to encode documents. (*CMOS*)

Text file
An informal term for a file that contains data encoded using ASCII. (*CMOS*)

TIFF, tiff, .tif*
Tagged Image File Format. A file format developed by Aldus and Microsoft and used to store bitmapped graphics including scanned line art and color images. (*CMOS*)

URL
Uniform Resource Locator. The global address of documents and other resources on the World Wide Web. Retrieved January 15, 2007 (http://www.webopedia.com/TERM/U/URL.html).

Web page
A virtual document delivered via the World Wide Web and viewed in a Web browser. (*CMOS*) Web browsers are software systems (such as Netscape Navigator and Microsoft Explorer) used to locate and display Web pages. Retrieved February 28, 2007 (http://www. webopedia.com/TERM/b/browser.html).

Web site
A site (location) on the World Wide Web. Each Web site contains a homepage, which is the first document users see when they enter a site. The site might also contain additional documents and files. Each site is owned and managed by an individual, company, or organization. Retrieved January 15, 2007 (http://www.webopedia. com/TERM/w/web_site.html).

World Wide Web
Also called the Web. The Internet's most widely used information-retrieval service. The World Wide Web uses Hypertext Transmission Protocol (HTTP) to allow users to request and retrieve documents (Web pages and multimedia objects) from other computers anywhere on the Internet. (*CMOS*)

5.2 The Internet

The Internet is a vast network of computers linked through interfaces such as the World Wide Web. The Web is the most common method social scientists use to access sources on the Internet, and although many sources (e.g., those in aggregated databases such as JSTOR, PsychInfo, HeinOnline) are the same as print-edition versions; others exist in a great variety of structures and formats. Nevertheless, the following basic rules apply:

- References (whether from print forms or online sources) should provide all basic elements of information about a source (name of author or institution, year of publication, name of article, title of publication, and name and location of publisher) so that the reader can access the material being cited.

- The sources (or versions of them) that are actually used are those that should be cited as references.

- Sources on the Internet that are not likely to change (e.g., those in PDF or TIFF form, those that are accessed through JSTOR, or those that are exact replicas of print-edition forms, such as newspapers) should be cited in print-form only instead of in ASCII, HTML, or other Web-based format versions. Even when citing PDF versions, however, use forms of citations that will be most widely accessible. Documents in these "non-changeable forms" may not be accessible for the following reasons:

- Some printed documents in electronic formats exist in databases that are subscription based and not widely available.

- Online newspapers and periodicals generally have a time limit for general access to some articles.

- Pursuant to court actions and other legal restrictions, some documents do not exist in electronic forms that are generally available.

• In all cases when using sources from the Internet, use names of authors (whenever possible), document titles, date of publication (or date of access or retrieval), and an address (such as a URL locator). The URL locator is critical in locating documents on the Internet. For example the ASA URL is http://www.asanet.org/.

• Because Web sites are modified, redesigned, updated, or deleted on an ongoing basis, it is important to take the following precautions:

- If a URL is cited, print and/or save in electronic form the data or document(s) obtained from it.

- Check spellings of URL addresses so that a source being cited is completely and accurately identified.

- Avoid citing documents in URL addresses that no longer exist by testing them before final submission of a manuscript.

- Do not type URL addresses: Use the copy function on a browser to transfer URL addresses to a manuscript.

5.3 Forms of Electronic References

5.3.1 E-Books

The form for citing e-books is the same as that used for citing print edition volumes, with the addition of information about the medium consulted. If an e-book was consulted online, the URL and date of access should also be cited (*CMOS* 2003:684–86):

> Spalter-Roth, Roberta, Norman Fortenberry, and Barbara Lovitts. 2007. *The Acceptance and Diffusion of Innovation: A Cross-Disciplinary Approach to Instructional and Curricular Change in Engineering.* Washington, DC: American Sociological Association. (Available on CD-ROM only.)

If a book is available in more than one format, other formats may be listed as well:

> Snyder, Howard N. and Melissa Sickmund. 2006. *Juvenile Offenders and Victims: 2006 National Report.* Pittsburgh, PA: National Center for Juvenile Justice. (Also available at http://ojjdp.ncjrs.gov/ojstatbb/nr2006/downloads/NR2006.pdf.)

5.3.2 Online Periodicals Available in Print and Online Form

The general form of online periodicals (including online journals, magazines, and newspapers) follows the pattern for all periodicals (see Section 4.3.2). If a print journal article is viewed in an online aggregate database such as JSTOR, indicate the database source and retrieval date as follows:

> Scott, Lionel D., Jr. and Laura E. House. 2005. "Relationship of Distress and Perceived Control to Coping with Perceived Racial Discrimination among Black Youth." *Journal of Black Psychology* 31(3):254–72. (Retrieved from JSTOR on December 16, 2006.)

5.3.3 Online Periodicals Available in Online Form Only

> Schafer, Daniel W. and Fred L. Ramsey. 2003. "Teaching the Craft of Data Analysis." *Journal of Statistics Education* 11(1). Retrieved December 12, 2006 (http://www.amstat.org/publications/jse/v11n1/schafer.html).

5.3.4 Web Sites

A general rule may be applied to the citing of Web sites: If the Web site contains data or evidence essential to a point being addressed in the manuscript, it should be formally cited with the URL and date of access.

- **Example 1:** A document retrieved from an institution with a known location:

  Text: (ASA 2006)

  Reference:
  American Sociological Association. 2006. "Status Committees." Washington, DC: American Sociological Association. Retrieved December 12, 2006 (http://www.asanet.org/cs/root/leftnav/committees/committees).

- **Example 2:** A report published in 2003 retrieved in January 2007 from a university Web site:

  Text: (Johns Hopkins University 2003)

  Reference:
  Johns Hopkins University. 2003. *Economic Impact of the Johns Hopkins Institutions in Maryland.* Silver Spring, MD: Johns Hopkins University and Johns Hopkins Medicine. Retrieved January 26, 2007 (http://www.jhu.edu/news_info/reports/impact/2003/impact2003.pdf).

- **Example 3:** A document retrieved from a corporate Web site (unknown location):

    Text: (IBM 2007)

    Reference:
    IBM. 2007. "Education: Solutions and Open Technologies for K–12 Schools, Higher Education and Lifelong Learning." Retrieved January 30, 2007 (http://www-3.ibm.com/industries/education/index.jsp?re=ibmhpdd).

5.3.5 Web Log Entries or Comments

The *ASA Style Guide* recommends the formal version of citing Web log (also known as "blogs") entries. If references to Web logs are included in a manuscript, they should be cited as follows:

    Text: (DeLong 2007)

    Reference:
    DeLong, Brad. 2007. "Thomas Piketty and Emmanuel Saez Give Their Current View on American Income Inequality." The Brad DeLong Blog, January 7, 2007. Retrieved January 9, 2007 (http://econ161.berkeley.edu/movable_type).

5.3.6 E-Mail Messages

If e-mails are referred to in a manuscript, they (like other personal communications) should be entered as part of the text and referenced in a footnote or endnote. E-mails are rarely cited in a reference list. When referring to communication by e-mail, obtain the permission of the owner before using it; do not cite the e-mail address.

    Text: In an e-mail message to the author, Jones indicated that was leaving the university.

    Footnote: [8] John Jones, e-mail message to author, May 23, 1999.

5.3.7 Items in Online Database

Journal articles published in online databases should be cited as shown in Section 5.3.2.

For references obtained from an online database, include the URL and an access date:

> *Text:* (National Center for Health Statistics 2007)
>
> *Reference:*
> National Center for Health Statistics. 2007. "Faststats, A to Z." Retrieved February 2, 2007 (http://www.cdc. gov/nchs/fastats/map_page.htm).

5.3.8 Data and Supporting Materials: Machine Readable Data Files (MRDF)

Researchers frequently cite data and related information (codekeys, statistical program information, variable lists) available in various Machine Readable Data Files (MRDF). These sources may be in either electronic media (CD-ROM, DVD, Magnetic tape) or downloaded from an online source. Examples of how to cite MRDF are included in Sections 11 and 12 (for online sources) of the Appendix.

5.4 Audiovisual Materials

5.4.1 CD-ROM or DVD-ROM

References to materials on CD-ROM are treated similarly to printed works (*CMOS* 2003:726). Place of publication may be omitted unless relevant.

5.4.2 Other Audiovisual Materials

For general guidelines for citations and references for other types of audiovisual media (film, sound recordings, slides, filmstrips, and videos), see *CMOS* 2003:724–27.

> Papademas, Dianne, ed. 2002. *Visual Sociology: Teaching with Film/Video, Photography, and Visual Media.* 5th

ed. VHS. Washington, DC: American Sociological Association.

JackDanyells. 2007. "TheYouTube Guided Tour." YouTube Web site. Retrieved February 2, 2007 (http://www.youtube.com).

Public Broadcasting Corporation (PBS). 2004. "Bill Moyers Talks with Ethicist Peter Singer." May 14, 2004. PBS Web site: NOW with Bill Moyers. This Week. Retrieved January 31, 2007 (http://www.pbs.org/now/thisweek/index_051404.html).

Library of Congress. 2007. "Addams, Jane. Photograph." Image (TIFF). Famous People: Selected Portraits from the Collections of the Library of Congress. Retrieved February 28, 2007 (http://lcweb2.loc.gov/master/pnp/cph/3a10000/3a13000/3a13000/3a13016u.tif).

Additional examples of preceding forms of e-resources are included in Sections 11 and 12 of the Appendix.

6 Preparing and Submitting a Manuscript to an ASA Journal

ASA journals have specific format requirements for manuscripts submitted to them for publication. Authors are advised to follow closely the guidelines listed below, because editors might return manuscripts that do not conform to these specifications. A checklist of elements required for submission is included in Section 6.6.

6.1 Keyboarding Specifications

6.1.1 Page Format

The checklists in Section 6.6 contain detailed specifications for page format requirements for manuscripts submitted to ASA journals in general. Authors are advised, however, to check with specific journals on guidelines for mechanics of submission (number of copies, policies on electronic submissions) and to verify details on issues such as submitting blinded versus unblinded copies.

6.1.2 Title Page

The title page should include the full title of the article, the name(s) and institution(s) of the author(s) (listed vertically if more than one), a running head, the word count for the manuscript (including footnotes and references), and a title footnote. An asterisk (*) following the title can be used to refer to the title footnote at the bottom of the page. This footnote includes the name and address of the corresponding author, acknowledgements, credits, and grant numbers.

Running Head = SHORTENED TITLE

**Full Title of the Article:
Capitalize Subtitle After Colon***

Author Full Name
Institution

Author Full Name
Institution

Word Count = Text, Footnotes, and References

* Title footnote includes name, address, and e-mail address
  of the corresponding author, as well as any acknowledgments, credits, and grant numbers

6.2 Submitting a Manuscript

Read and revise a manuscript multiple times. Before sending it to a journal, read the manuscript one more time. Then
package it securely and include the following:

- A **cover letter** giving the address, phone and fax numbers,
  and e-mail address of the corresponding author; the title
  of the manuscript; and any other important information,
  such as changes of address and availability.

- **Four (4) copies of the manuscript**, including title page,
  abstract, text, footnotes, appendices, references, tables,
  and figures, illustrations, and photographs with titles.
  (*Note:* The number of copies may vary among different
  ASA journals.)

- An **electronic copy of the manuscript** is highly recommended but not required. Submission of an electronic
  copy will allow the manuscript to be sent for review
  electronically and will reduce the length of time required

for the review process. The electronic copy of the manuscript, which must be prepared using standard word processing software (e.g., MS Word or WordPerfect), may be forwarded to the editorial office as an e-mail attachment or in some other electronic media format. Exceptions to these word processing or media formats must be cleared with editors of journals before submission.

- A check for the **$25 manuscript processing fee,** made payable to the American Sociological Association. No fee is required for papers authored by ASA student members.

- Processing fees are *not* required for comments, replies, or revise-resubmits. Submit **comments on previously published articles** directly to the journal.

- *Reminder:* **Double-space** all text in the abstract, text, references, footnotes, and acknowledgments; block quotations may be single spaced. All text must be in 12-point Times New Roman type (Times is also acceptable).

6.3 Ethical Guidelines

The American Sociological Association regards the submission of a manuscript to more than one professional journal at the same time as an unethical practice. Manuscripts that have appeared or will appear in whole or part in other publications must be clearly identified as such. All persons who publish in ASA journals are required to abide by the *ASA Code of Ethics* regarding plagiarism, authorship credit, and other ethical issues. See the *ASA Code of Ethics* available online at http://www.asanet.org.

6.4 Copyright

ASA holds copyright on all materials published in ASA journals, although material published in 1964 or earlier is now in the public domain. Should a manuscript be accepted for publication, an author will be required to transfer the copyright to the ASA. After an article has been published, an author may use it without charge or permission in any future printed book or article of which that author is the sole author or editor.

6.5 Formatting a Manuscript for Publication

If a manuscript is accepted for publication, an author may be asked to provide manuscript materials as electronic computer files. Some generally accepted software program for text and graphics are listed below. Contact the journal office to confirm that a particular software format or computer file is acceptable.

Text

For manuscript text (body of manuscript, biography, references, etc.), MS Word or WordPerfect is preferred.

Tables

Preferred table programs are MS Word (table function) or Excel. Lines (called "rules") within a table should be at least 1/2 point or thicker. (Do not use hairline rules, which are too fine for print production.) Tables should be embedded within the electronic manuscript file.

Journal Page Size

For most ASA journals, the page of a bound print journal is smaller that a regular piece of letter-size (8.5" by 11") paper. All text, tables, and figures are typeset and sized to fit this journal page dimension. When figures are sized down to fit on the page, any text or type in the actual figure should not be smaller than 8-point Times New Roman font in the final printed journal page. For example, an Excel chart/graph that is to be reduced to 55 percent in the print journal article should use 14.5 Times New Roman font in the original (100 percent size) Excel chart/graph file.

For tables, all the text and/or data should fit on the print journal page (vertically) across two columns. If the table is too wide for the journal page, it will be typeset as a broadside table (oriented 90 degrees from original) on the page. Please refer to a recent issue of the journal to see how tables and figures have been typeset previously.

Disks and CDs

For the accepted manuscript, send the journal office the disk/CD that contains the computer file of the figure as created in the original program (e.g., an Excel graphic must be sent as an Excel file, not pasted into a Word document file). Do not send laser proofs; they do not reproduce well in print composition. Sending a word-processing document with a figure placed in it is not useful unless the original graphic file is also sent as a separate file (see previous paragraph).

Figures and Graphics

Send only black-and-white figures; do not send color figures. When available, send the computer file of the figures. Some journal offices may prefer Excel (*.xls) computer files for graphs/charts. For other illustrations and images, acceptable programs include Photoshop, PowerPoint, Illustrator, Freehand, or Corel Draw. Preferred formats for illustrations, images, and photos are *.tif files using grayscale (not CMYK) with LZW compression, or *.eps files (not *.ps files). *Do not* send files from StATA and Paint; these are not suitable for graphics for print. Authors can convert StATA files to Excel and then submit the Excel file. Contact the journal office to confirm that the software or computer file is acceptable.

Provide the original computer file(s) of the figure(s) as created in the original program (e.g., an Excel chart/graph must be sent as an Excel file), not pasted or inserted into a Word document file. Do not send a figure placed in a word-processing document; this is not useful because the word-processing document contains only a low-resolution 72 dpi preview.

Use at least 300 dpi resolution for grayscale (not CMYK); use at least 600 dpi resolution for line art (1200 dpi is preferred). Do not send 72 dpi "screen shots" or Web gifs because while they appear clear on a computer screen, they will reproduce very badly in print form.

Lines (called "rules") within a figure (chart/graph), at reduction size, must be at least 1/2 point or thicker. (Do not use hairline rules, which are too fine for print production). For example, if the chart/graph will be printed in the journal at 55 percent reduction, the original (100 percent) size of the rule should be at least 1 point to appear in the journal at 1/2 point.

A note about Excel graphs/charts: Excel is the preferred program for figures, graphs, and charts in some journal offices. When creating or generating a chart in Excel, be sure to designate the "chart location" in the Excel file "As new sheet." Name this new sheet Figure 1, etc. All the data for the figure(s) can appear on one worksheet, but do not make the graph/chart an object within that same data worksheet (i.e., do not designate the chart location for the graph/chart "As object in"; locate each figure "As new sheet").

Authors who choose to send reflective art, should send veloxes, PMTs (photo mechanical transfer), or Photostats instead of laser printouts. If the illustration contains grays, a continuous tone print is preferred. Authors should also consider the size that an illustration will be reduced to in the published print article. For example, if an illustration will be reduced 50 percent in print, the finest rule in a 100 percent original should be 1 point, which will reduce to 1/2 point at the print size. If you must send a laser proof of an illustration that contains grays, do not use the printer's default screen. The screen, at the final print size, must be no finer than 133 line (e.g., if an illustration will reduce to 50 percent in print, a laser proof's screen must be no finer than 66.5).

Consistency of Type (Font) Size

To ensure that the type sizes are the same in all the figures in the print journal page, the author or artist needs to compute the inverse of the focus of the reproduction size of the image and size the type (font) in the original accordingly.

6.6 Checklist for Preparing and Submitting a Manuscript to an ASA Journal

For more specific information on any of following issues, review the contents of Section 6 in the *ASA Style Guide*. See also *The Chicago Manual of Style* (2003:59, 68–69); "Electronic Manuscript Preparation Guidelines for Authors," available at http://www.press.uchicago.edu/Misc/Chicago/emsguide.html; and "Preparation Checklist for ASA Manuscripts," available at http://www.asanet.org/galleries/default-file/asaguidelinesnew.pdf.

Check for items shown on the following pages:

6.6.1 Keyboarding the Manuscript

- ❏ **Double-space text** (including references, footnotes, and endnotes).
  - Text must be in **12-point Times New Roman (Times** is also acceptable).
  - **Block quotes may be single-spaced.**
- ❏ **Create margins of 1.25 inches** on all four sides to allow room for the editor's or copyeditor's marks.
- ❏ **Number all pages** sequentially.
- ❏ **Remove comments** or other hidden text; accept all tracked changes as final (i.e., there should be nothing hidden in the manuscript).
- ❏ **Avoid using space bars or indents** to achieve tabs, align text, or create hanging indents.
- ❏ **Avoid using the automatic hyphen feature.**
- ❏ **Do not right-justify text.**
- ❏ **Use only "normal" settings.** (Do not assign different styles for headings, block quotations, etc.)
- ❏ **Create block quotations using the word-processing feature** for indenting paragraphs. Use one hard return at the end of the quotation block.
- ❏ Produce **special characters** using only the word-processing program's built-in character set (i.e., do not create characters from characters on the keyboard).
- ❏ **Use a hard return after the following:**
  - Title of the article
  - Running heads
  - Each paragraph
  - Each text heading
  - Each page heading (e.g., Abstract, Biography, Table titles)

- Each reference
- Each footnote

☐ Use *italic* type for variables in mathematical equations and text; use ***bold italic*** type to indicate vectors or matrices in equations and text. (See *CMOS* 2003:526.)

☐ **Place footnotes or endnotes as text at the end of the manuscript.** Footnotes and endnotes in the text must be indicated by superscripted numbers.

6.6.2 Checking the Manuscript Content

☐ Run **spell check and grammar check**. (Authors should note that these functions may not always be reliable.)

☐ Check all **headings and subheadings** for consistency and accuracy. Are headings formatted correctly for all levels? Do titles accurately reflect content and organization of the paper?

☐ Check for **subject–verb agreement** and **parallel grammatical structures.**

☐ Cite all **attributions** to other publications and works fully, appropriately, and accurately.

☐ Check accuracy of form and content of **references cited in text.**

☐ Check that all **text citations have references and vice versa** (i.e., drop any references not cited in text).

☐ Check that all **references follow ASA style guidelines.**

☐ Check that references are **alphabetized.**

☐ Proof **accuracy of references** (names, titles of articles, publications, page numbers, etc.).

☐ Be sensitive to **"blinding"** the manuscript for reviewers by removing all identifying information throughout the manuscript.

- ❑ Proof **tables and figures for accuracy**.
- ❑ **Cross-check:**
  - **Illustrations against captions, text references, and callouts** (places in text indicating placement of illustration)
  - **Figures and tables with data references in text; tables against table lists, and tables against callouts** (places in text indicating placement of tables)
  - **All cross-references**
  - All **URLs cited and all electronic links** (be sure they work).

6.6.3 Submitting the Manuscript

When submitting the manuscript to an editorial office, include the following:

- ❑ A **title page**, including:
  - Full title of the article
  - Names and institutions for all authors (listed vertically if there is more than one author)
  - Running head (60 characters or less)
  - Approximate word count for the manuscript
  - Title footnote
  - Asterisk (*) by the title refers to the title footnote at the bottom of the title page. The title footnote includes the name and address of the corresponding author, acknowledgments, credits, and grant information.

- ❑ **Abstract,** which is
  - On a separate page headed by a title
  - Brief (one paragraph, no more than 200 words) and descriptive (a summary of the most important contributions in a paper)
  - Accessible (jargon-free and clear to the general reader)
  - A good test: Can it serve as a press release about the research?

- ☐ A **cover letter** giving the address, phone and fax numbers, and e-mail address of the corresponding author; the title of the manuscript; and any other important information, such as changes of address and availability.

- ☐ **Four (4) copies of the manuscript**, including title page, abstract, text, footnotes, appendices, references, tables, and figures, illustrations, and photographs with titles. (*Note:* The number of copies may vary among different ASA journals.)

- ☐ **Appendices:**
  - Label appendices *Appendix A*, *Appendix B*, etc. Appendices appear at the end of an article (after references).
  - Cross-check text for accuracy against appendices.

- ☐ **Tables:**
  - Number tables consecutively throughout the text.
  - Print or type tables and include them at the end of the manuscript. Insert a note in the text to indicate table placement (*TABLE 2 ABOUT HERE*).
  - Place each table on a separate page.
  - Include a descriptive title and headings for all columns and rows on each table.

- ☐ **Figures, illustrations, photographs, and other graphic materials:**
  - Number them consecutively throughout the text.
  - Include a title for each figure, illustration, and photograph. Each must be labeled clearly.
  - Insert a note in text to indicate placement (*FIGURE 1 ABOUT HERE*).

- ☐ **Permissions** that may be required to reproduce illustrations or previously published materials.

- ☐ If electronic versions of text are being sent with printed copies, **printed and electronic copies must be exactly**

the same. (Do not make any changes on the disk after printing the final manuscript.) (Authors should keep one copy in the same form.)

❏ **Disks that are labeled and dated** (including the name of the software used to produce the manuscript—e.g., Corel WordPerfect Version 10, or MS Word 2002 for Windows XP).

❏ **Biography** (five or six lines for each author), including:
- Author's name, title, department, institution
- A brief description of current research interests, publications, or awards

❏ A check for the **manuscript processing fee,** made payable to the American Sociological Association. No fee is required for papers authored by ASA student members.

7 Interpreting Copyeditors' Notations

If a manuscript is accepted for publication, a copyeditor will edit it using the following standard proofreading marks:

Changes to Text

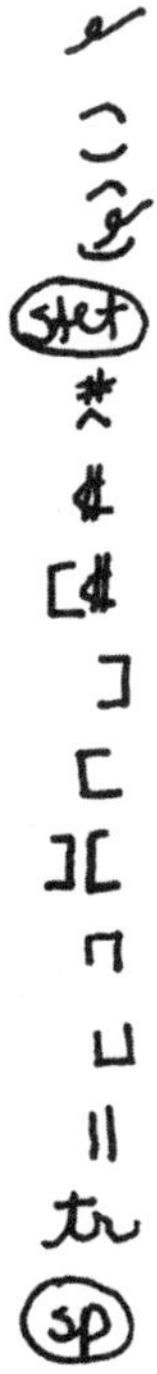

�	Delete
⌒	Close up; delete space
⌒̸	Delete and close up (for letters within a word)
 (stet)	Let it stand as is
#	Insert space
¶	New paragraph
[¶	Flush paragraph
]	Move to the right; indent
[	Move to the left; to left margin
][	Center
⊓	Move up
⊔	Move down
‖	Align vertically
tr	Transpose
 (sp)	Spell out

Type Specifications

(ital)	Italic type
(rom)	Roman (not bold or italic) type
(bf)	Bold type
(lc)	Lowercase letters
(uc)	Uppercase letters
⌄2	Superscript
⌃2	Subscript
m̲̲	Capitalize

Punctuation

⌄	Insert comma
⌄	Insert apostrophe or single quotation mark
⌄⌄	Insert quotation marks
⊙	Insert period
⊙⊙⊙	Insert ellipses
;|	Insert semicolon
⌄ or :|	Insert colon
/	Insert virgule (slash)
⹀	Insert hyphen
⊥/m	Insert em dash
⊥/n	Insert en dash
(|)	Insert parentheses
[|]	Insert brackets

8 References and Other Sources

8.1 References

American Educational Research Association. 2007. "Standards for Reporting on Empirical Social Science Research in AERA Publications." *Educational Researcher* 35(6):33–40. (Also available at http://www.aera.net/uploadedFiles/Publications/Journals/Educational_Researcher/3506/12ERv35n6_Standard4Report%20.pdf.)

The American Heritage Dictionary of the English Language. 4th ed. 2000. New York: Bartleby.Com. Retrieved December 15, 2006 (http://www.bartleby.com/61/).

American Psychological Association. 2001. *Publication Manual of the American Psychological Association.* 5th ed. Washington, DC: American Psychological Association.

———. 2006. "Electronic References." Washington, DC: American Psychological Association. Retrieved December 12, 2006 (http://www.apastyle.org/elecref.html).

American Sociological Association. 2006a. *ASA Code of Ethics.* Washington, DC: American Sociological Association. Retrieved December 18, 2006 (http://www.asanet.org).

———. 2006b. "The Preparation Checklist for ASA Manuscripts." Washington, DC: American Sociological Association. Retrieved December 16, 2006 (http://www.asanet.org/galleries/default-file/asaguidelinesnew.pdf).

———. 2006c. "A Quick Style Guide for Students Writing Sociology Papers." Washington, DC: American Sociological Association. Retrieved December 16, 2007 (http://www.asanet.org/page.ww?name=Quick+Style+Guide&section=Sociology+Depts).

Becker, Howard. 1986. *Writing for Social Scientists*. Chicago, IL: University of Chicago Press.

Day, Robert A. and Barbara Gastel. 2006. *How to Write and Publish a Scientific Paper*. 6th ed. Westport, CT: Greenwood Press.

Harvard Law Review Association. 2000. *The Bluebook: A Uniform System of Citation*. 17th ed. Cambridge, MA: Harvard Law Review Association.

Library of Congress. 2007. THOMAS. Retrieved December 17, 2006 (http://thomas.loc.gov/).

Merriam-Webster's Collegiate Dictionary. 2005. 11th ed. Springfield, MA: Merriam-Webster.

Merriam-Webster Online. 2007. Springfield, MA: Merriam-Webster. Retrieved January 9, 2007 (http://www.m-w.com/).

Strunk, William F., Jr. and E. B. White. 2000. *The Elements of Style*. 4th ed. New York: Macmillan.

The University of Chicago Press. 2003. *The Chicago Manual of Style*. 15th ed. Chicago, IL: University of Chicago Press.

————. 2006a. "Chicago-Style Citation Quick Guide." Retrieved December 16, 2006 (http://www.chicagomanualofstyle.org/tools_citationguide.html).

————. 2006b. "Electronic Manuscript Preparation Guidelines for Authors." Retrieved December 16, 2006 (http://www.press.uchicago.edu/Misc/Chicago/emsguide.html).

Webopedia. 2007. Darien, CT: Jupitermedia Inc. Retrieved January 18, 2007 (http://www.webopedia.com).

Williams, Joseph M. 2007. *Style: Lessons in Clarity and Grace*. 9th ed. New York: Pearson Longman.

8.2 Other Sources

The references listed below are widely used in the social sciences:

Evans, Bergen and Cornelia Evans. [1957] 2000. *A Dictionary of Contemporary American Usage*. New York: Random House.

Fowler, H. W. 1965. *A Dictionary of Modern English Usage*. 2nd ed. New York: Oxford University Press.

Gibaldi, Joseph. 1998. *MLA Style Manual and Guide to Scholarly Publishing*. 2nd ed. New York: Modern Language Association of America.

———. 2003. *MLA Handbook for Writers of Research Papers*. 6th ed. New York: Modern Language Association of America.

Merriam-Webster Concise Handbook for Writers. 1998. 2nd ed. Springfield, MA: Merriam-Webster.

Merriam-Webster Thesaurus. 2005. Springfield, MA: Merriam Webster.

Mullins, Carolyn J. [1977] 1984. *A Guide to Writing and Publishing in the Social and Behavioral Sciences*. New York: John Wiley and Sons.

Skillin, Marjorie E., with Robert M. Gay et al. 1974. *Words into Type*. 3rd ed. Englewood Cliffs, NJ: Prentice-Hall.

Swanson, Ellen. 1999. *Mathematics into Type*. Updated ed. Providence, RI: American Mathematical Society.

Theodorson, George A. and Achilles G. Theodorson. [1969] 1979. *A Modern Dictionary of Sociology*. 11th ed. New York: Barnes and Noble.

Zinsser, William. [1976] 2001. *On Writing Well*. New York: Harper and Row.

Appendix

Reference List Formats: Some Examples

1. Books

See Section 4.3.2 for explanation and additional examples.

Mason, Karen O. 1974. *Women's Labor Force Participation and Fertility*. Research Triangle Park, NC: National Institutes of Health.

Edelman, Peter, Harry J. Holzer, and Paul Offner. 2006. *Reconnecting Disadvantaged Young Men*. Washington, DC: Urban Institute Press.

Berlin, Gorden and Andrew Sum. 1988. *Toward a More Perfect Union: Basic Skills, Poor Families, and Our Economic Future*. New York: Ford Foundation.

Editions of Books

McCullagh, Peter and John A. Nedler. 1989. *Generalized Linear Models*. 2nd ed. London, England: Chapman and Hall.

Note: The abbreviation for 2nd is now preferred (*CMOS* 2003:381, 665); some other possible abbreviations for editions: Rev. ed., 2 vols., 3rd ed.

Volumes of Books

Gurr, Ted Robert, ed. 1989. *Violence in America*. Vol. 1, *The History of Crime*. Newbury Park, CA: Sage Publications.

Thirsk, Joan, ed. 1984. *The Agrarian History of England and Wales*. Vol. 5, *1640–1750*. Cambridge, England: Cambridge University Press.

Translations

Barbagli, Marzio. 1982. *Educating for Unemployment: Politics, Labor Markets, and the School System—Italy, 1959–1973*. Translated by R. H. Ross. New York: Columbia University Press.

Lattimore, Richmond, trans. 1951. *The Iliad of Homer*. Chicago, IL: University of Chicago Press.

Note: The second example suggests an alternate form for citing translated works.

Compilations

Russell, Katheryn K., Heather L. Pfeifer, and Judith L. Jones, comp. 2000. *Race and Crime: An Annotated Bibliography*. Westport, CT: Greenwood Press.

Edited Volumes

Leonard, Kimberly Kempf, Carl E. Pope, and William H. Feyerherm, eds. 1995. *Minorities in Juvenile Justice*. Thousand Oaks, CA: Sage Publications.

Koshar, Rudy, ed. 1990. *Splintered Classes*. New York: Holmes and Meier.

Republished Works

Bernard, Claude. [1865] 1957. *An Introduction to the Study of Experimental Medicine*. Translated by H. C. Greene. Reprint, New York: Dover.

Goldman, Emma. [1914] 1987. *The Social Significance of the Modern Drama*. Reprint, New York: Applause.

2. Chapters from Books, Articles from Collected Works

See Section 4.3.2 for explanation and additional examples.

Palacios, Wilson R., Chinita Heard, and Dorothy L. Taylor. 2003. "At a Crossroad: Affirmative Action and Criminology." Pp. 415–29 in *Crime Control and Social Justice: The Delicate Balance*, edited by D. F. Hawkins, S. L. Myers, Jr., and R. N. Stone. Westport, CT: Greenwood Press.

Clausen, John A. 1972. "The Life Course of Individuals." Pp. 457–514 in *Aging and Society*. Vol. 3, *A Sociology of Age Stratification*, edited by M. W. Riley, M. Johnson, and A. Foner. New York: Russell Sage.

Note: The form of citing volume number in collected works has changed in the third edition of the *ASA Style Guide* (See Section 4.3.2).

3. Articles from Journals

See Section 4.3.2 for explanation and additional examples.

Fine, Gary Alan and Kent Sandstrom. 1993. "Ideology in Action: A Pragmatic Approach to a Contested Concept." *Sociological Theory* 11:21–38.

Pescosolido, Bernice A. and Melissa A. Milkie. 1995. "The Status of Teacher Training in U.S. and Canadian Sociology Departments." *Teaching Sociology* 23:341–52.

Sampson, Robert J., Jeffrey D. Morenoff, and Felton Earls. 1999. "Beyond Social Capital: Spatial Dynamics of Collective Efficacy for Children." *American Sociological Review* 64:633–60.

Goodman, Leo A. 1947a. "The Analysis of Systems of Qualitative Variables When Some of the Variables Are Unobservable. Part I—A Modified Latent Structure Approach." *American Journal of Sociology* 79:1179–259.

———. 1947b. "Exploratory Latent Structure Analysis Using Both Identifiable and Unidentifiable Models." *Biometrika* 61:215–31.

Conger, Rand D. Forthcoming. "The Effects of Positive Feedback on Direction and Amount of Verbalization in a Social Setting." *Sociological Perspectives.*

Note: The preceding examples do not include the issue number of the journal. The form (when the journal issue is included) should be as follows, where *(2)* represents the issue number:

Kalleberg, Arne L., Barbara F. Reskin, and Ken Hudson. 2000. "Bad Jobs in America: Standard and Nonstandard Employment Relations and Job Quality in the United States." *American Sociological Review* 65(2):256–78.

Articles Published in More Than One Journal

Patch, C. Ross. 1985–1986. "The Next to Last Angry Man," parts 1–3. *World's End Review* 8:315–30; 9:27–52, 125–42.

Articles from Foreign-Language Journals

Kenny, Martin and Richard Florida. 1989. "Response to the Debate over 'Beyond Madd Production'" (in Japanese). *Mado* 83:120–45.

Wegener, Berndt. 1987. "Von Nutzen Entfernter Bekannter" (Benefiting from Persons We Barely Know). *Kölner Zeitschrift für Soziologie und Sozialpsychologie* 39:278–301.

4. Articles from Newspapers and Magazines

Guiles, Melinda and Krystal Miller. 1990. "Mazda and Mitsubishi-Chrysler Venture Cut Output, Following Big Three's Lead." *Wall Street Journal,* January 12, pp. A2, A12.

Anderson, Elijah. 1994. "The Code of the Streets." *Atlantic Monthly*, May 1994, pp. 81–94.

Duke, Lynne. 1994. "Confronting Violence: African American Conferees Look Inward." *Washington Post*, January 8, pp. A1, A10.

5. Archival Sources

George Meany Memorial Archives, Legislature Reference Files, Box 6. March 18, 1970. File: 20. Memo, Conference with Gloster Current, Director of Organization, National Association for the Advancement of Colored People.

National Archives, Record Group 174, Box 144. 1964. File: State and Local Promotion, January-February 1964. Letter from the President of the United Association of Journeymen and Apprentices of the Plumbing and Pipe Fitting Industry to Willard Wirtz.

Note: If a manuscript refers to large numbers of archival sources, group them together in a separate section of the references headed "Archival Sources."

6. Government Documents

Bonczar, Thomas P. and Allen J. Beck. 1997. *Lifetime Likelihood of Going to State or Federal Prison.* Bureau of Justice Statistics Special Bulletin, NCJ 160092. Washington, DC: U.S. Department of Justice.

General Accounting Office. 1990. *Death Penalty Sentencing: Research Indicates Pattern of Racial Disparities.* GGD-90–57. Washington, DC: General Accounting Office.

U.S. Congress. 1950. House Subcommittee on the Study of Monopoly Power of the Committee on the Judiciary. *Study of Monopoly Power:* Hearing. 81st Congress, 2nd Session, pp. 788–91.

U.S. Bureau of the Census. 1960. *Characteristics of Population.* Vol. 1. Washington, DC: U.S. Government Printing Office.

U.S. Department of Justice. Bureau of Justice Statistics. 1984. *Criminal Victimization in the U.S., 1983.* Washington, DC: U.S. Government Printing Office.

U.S. Department of Justice. Federal Bureau of Investigation. 2004. *Crime in the United States, 2003: Uniform Crime Reports.* Washington, DC: Government Printing Office. (Also available at (http://www.fbi.gov/ucr/ucr.htm.)

7. Dissertations and Theses

King, Andrew J. 1976. "Law and Land Use in Chicago: A Pre-History of Modern Zoning." PhD dissertation, Department of Sociology, University of Wisconsin, Madison, WI.

8. Unpublished Papers

Nomiya, Daishiro. 1988. "Urbanization and Income Inequality: A Cross-National Study." Department of Sociology, University of North Carolina, Chapel Hill, NC. Unpublished manuscript.

9. Working and Discussion Papers

Dickens, William T. and Kevin Lang. 1985. "Testing Dual Labor Market Theory: A Reconsideration of the Evidence." Working Paper No. 1670, National Bureau of Economic Research, Chicago, IL.

Sørensen, Aage B. 1983. "Processes of Allocation to Open and Closed Positions in Social Structure." Discussion Paper No. 722–83, Institute for Research on Poverty, University of Wisconsin, Madison, WI.

10. Presented Papers

Zerubavel, Eviatar. 1978. "The Benedictine Ethic and the Spirit of Scheduling." Presented at the annual meeting of the International Society for the Comparative Study of Civilizations, April 22, Milwaukee, WI.

11. Machine-Readable Data Files

American Institute of Public Opinion. 1976. *Gallup Public Opinion Poll # 965* [MRDF]. Princeton, NJ: American Institute of Public Opinion [producer]. New Haven, CT: Roper Public Opinion Research Center, Yale University [distributor].

U.S. Bureau of the Census. 1970. *Census of Population and Housing 1970, Summary Statistic File 4H: U.S.* [MRDF]. DUALabs ed. Washington, DC: U.S. Bureau of the Census [producer]. Rosslyn, VA: Data Use and Access laboratories (DUALabs) [distributor].

12. E-Resources

Books

Book: Selected chapter(s) (available online)

Edelman, Peter, Harry J. Holzer, and Paul Offner. 2006. *Reconnecting Disadvantaged Young Men*, An Introduction. Retrieved December 12, 2006 (http://www.urban.org/expert.cfm?ID=PeterEdelman).

Book: Available online with suggested citation (two tables)

Pastore, Ann L. and Kathleen Maguire, eds. 2003. *Sourcebook of Criminal Justice Statistics*. Retrieved June 30, 2006 (http://www.albany.edu/sourcebook/pdf/t212.pdf; http://www.albany.edu/sourcebook/pdf/t226.pdf).

Journal Articles

If a print journal article is viewed in an online aggregate database such as JSTOR, indicate the database source and retrieval date according to the following example:

Scott, Lionel D., Jr. and Laura E. House. 2005. "Relationship of Distress and Perceived Control to Coping with Perceived Racial Discrimination among Black Youth." *Journal of Black Psychology* 31(3):254–72. (Retrieved from JSTOR on December 16, 2006.)

Snyder, Howard N. and Melissa Sickmund. 2006. *Juvenile Offenders and Victims: 2006 National Report.* Pittsburgh, PA: National Center for Juvenile Justice. (Also available at http://ojjdp.ncjrs.gov/ojstatbb/nr2006/downloads/ NR2006.pdf.)

Journal article that exists only in an e-journal (online access only)

Schafer, Daniel W. and Fred L. Ramsey. 2003. "Teaching the Craft of Data Analysis." *Journal of Statistics Education* 11(1). Retrieved December 12, 2006 (http://www. amstat.org/publications/jse/v11n1/schafer.html).

Reports, Bulletins, Fact Sheets, and Newsletters

Report: Online version (no author)

U.S. Department of Justice. Bureau of Justice Statistics. 2006. "Key Crime & Justice Facts at a Glance." (Revised December 10, 2006.) Retrieved December 12, 2006 (http://www.ojp.usdoj.gov/bjs/glance.htm).

Report: Online version (with author or with suggested citations)

Catalano, Shannan M. 2006. *National Crime Victimization Survey: Criminal Victimization, 2005.* Bureau of Justice Statistics: Bulletin. Washington, DC: U.S. Department of Justice. Retrieved December 12, 2006 (http://www.ojp.usdoj.gov/bjs/pub/ascii/cv05.txt).

Newsletter with author (online access only)

Howery, Carla B. 2006. "New Annual Meeting Workshops Designed for Practitioner Networking." *Footnotes*, November. Retrieved December 12, 2006 (http://www2.asanet.org/footnotes/nov06/fn4.html).

Newsletter with no author (print and online access):

American Sociological Association. 2004. "Public Affairs Update: Concerned Scientists Say Bush Administration Ignores Research . . . ." *Footnotes*, April. Retrieved December 12, 2006 (http://www2.asanet.org/footnotes/apr04/).

Newspapers and Magazines

Sampson, Robert J. 2006. "Open Doors Don't Invite Criminals." *New York Times*, March 11. Retrieved March 11, 2006 (http://www.nyt.com).

Online Databases, Spreadsheets, and Code Books

Tables in PDF or XLS Spreadsheet format

Scientists and Engineers Statistical Data System (SESTAT). 2006. "Table B-1: U.S. Scientists and Engineers, by Detailed Field and Level of Highest Degree Attained: 1999." Retrieved December 12, 2006 (http://srsstats.sbe.nsf.gov/preformatted-tables/1999/tables/TableB1.pdf).

Survey instrument

U.S. Bureau of the Census. 1999. "1999 Survey of Doctorate Recipients." Washington, DC: U.S. Department of Commerce. Retrieved December 12, 2006 (http://srsstats.sbe.nsf.gov/docs/sdr99.pdf).

Web Site (No Author)

American Anthropological Association. 2006. "Race." Retrieved December 12, 2006 (http://raceproject.aaanet.org).

Web Log (Blog)

DeLong, Brad. 2007. "Thomas Piketty and Emmanuel Saez Give Their Current View on American Income Inequality." The Brad DeLong Blog, January 7, 2007. Retrieved January 9, 2007 (http://econ161.berkeley.edu/movable_type).